# THE DEFENSE OF JISR AL-DOREAA

With E. D. Swinton's *The Defence of Duffer's Drift*

**FOREWORD BY JOHN A. NAGL**

*Senior Fellow, Center for a New American Security*

THE UNIVERSITY OF CHICAGO PRESS • *Chicago and London*

# THE DEFENSE OF

MICHAEL L. BURGOYNE

*and*

ALBERT J. MARCKWARDT

# JISR AL-DOREAA

**Captain Michael Burgoyne** was deployed in 2003 in support of Operation Iraqi Freedom as a squadron logistics officer, working across 14,000 square kilometers of contested terrain in al-Anbar Province, Iraq. In 2005 he commanded C Troop, Third Squadron, 7th U.S. Cavalry, and conducted hundreds of missions across Iraq from al-Qiam to southeast Baghdad, including the first Iraqi parliamentary election. He has also served as a troop/company trainer at the National Training Center at Fort Irwin, California.

**Captain Albert J. Marckwardt** was deployed in 2005 in support of Operation Iraqi Freedom as a squadron logistics officer for Third Squadron, 7th U.S. Cavalry, supporting missions throughout eastern Baghdad. Deployed for a second time in 2007 as part of the "surge," Captain Marckwardt commanded B Troop, Third Squadron, 7th U.S. Cavalry, where he controlled the densely populated and volatile Adhamiyah region in the heart of Baghdad. He now serves as aide-de-camp to the commanding general, Third Infantry Division.

The University of Chicago Press, Chicago 60637
The University of Chicago Press, Ltd., London
© 2009 by The University of Chicago
Foreword © 2009 by John A. Nagl
All rights reserved. Published 2009
Printed in the United States of America

18 17 16 15 14 13 12                    3 4 5

ISBN-13: 978-0-226-08092-5   (cloth)
ISBN-13: 978-0-226-08093-2   (paper)

ISBN-10: 0-226-08092-7   (cloth)
ISBN-10: 0-226-08093-5   (paper)

Library of Congress Cataloging-in-Publication Data
Burgoyne, Michael L.
    The defense of Jisr al-Doreaa : with E.D. Swinton's the Defence of Duffer's Drift /
  Michael L. Burgoyne and Albert J. Marckwardt ; with a foreword by John A. Nagl.
    p. cm.
    Includes bibliographical references.
    ISBN-13: 978-0-226-08092-5 (hbk. : alk. paper)
    ISBN-10: 0-226-08092-7 (hbk. : alk. paper)
    ISBN-13: 978-0-226-08093-2 (pbk. : alk. paper)
    ISBN-10: 0-226-08093-5 (pbk. : alk. paper)
    1. Counterinsurgency.  2. Guerrilla warfare.  3. Tactics.  4. Iraq War, 2003-  5.
  South African War, 1899–1902.  6. Didactic literature.  I. Marckwardt, Albert
  J.  II. Swinton, E. D. (Ernest Dunlop), 1868–1951. Defence of Duffer's Drift.
  III. Title.  IV. Title: E.D. Swinton's the Defence of Duffer's Drift.  V. Title:
  Defence of Duffer's Drift.
  U241.B87 2008
  355.02'18—dc22

                                                            2008040133

*Photo credits*—US Soldiers, p. x: photograph courtesy of SFC Dillard Johnson.
Iraqi soldier on truck, p. 71: photographer unknown, 2005; courtesy of the authors.
Multinational patrols, p. 72: photograph by Albert J. Marckwardt, 2007.

∞ The paper used in this publication meets the minimum requirements of the
American National Standard for Information Sciences—Permanence of Paper for
Printed Library Materials, ANSI Z39.48-1992.

# CONTENTS

# FOREWORD

From 1899 to 1902, the British army fought a very difficult campaign against the Boers (Dutch for "farmer") in South Africa. Although initially unprepared for the colonial warfare they confronted, the Brits adapted, learned, and ultimately defeated their insurgent enemies in a pattern they would follow repeatedly in a series of colonial wars.

A small classic of the Boer War is the book by then captain Ernest D. Swinton entitled *The Defence of Duffer's Drift*. A drift is a small hill; Duffer's Drift controlled an important river crossing, and Lieutenant Backsight Forethought struggles with its tactical defense against his insurgent enemies. "Now, if they had given me a job like fighting the Battle of Waterloo, or Sedan, or Bull Run, I knew all about that," he thinks, but this much smaller battle is a challenge that at first defeats him. Given the opportunity to fight over and over again in a kind of *Groundhog Day* scenario, Backsight Forethought eventually triumphs; the story of how he manages to learn tactical lessons has inspired literally generations of British and American officers since.

In fact, U.S. Army Colonel James R. McDonough followed E. D. Swinton's script in his 1993 book, *The Defense of Hill 781*, which analyzes the performance of Lieutenant Colonel A. Tack Always in mechanized battle at the National Training Center in Fort Irwin, California. One can picture the long-dead Major General Swinton—perhaps the one man most responsible for the invention

of the main battle tank in World War I and later commandant of the Royal Tank Corps—looking down from
Valhalla, twirling his moustaches and wearing a pleased
expression indeed.

Unfortunately, the National Training Center was the
wrong place to learn lessons of future war; better for
soldiers to have read *Platoon Leader*, McDonough's
book on his experience in Vietnam. (In the wake of that
war, the army focused all but exclusively on conventional
combat at the National Training Center.)

Many of the lessons learned by Backsight Forethought
appear in the 2006 *U.S. Army/Marine Corps Counterinsurgency Field Manual*, which explicitly posits the need
to "learn and adapt" to the demands of modern warfare.
The manual played an important role in the switch to
a new counterinsurgency strategy in Iraq championed
by General David Petraeus, but many young officers
struggled with the implementation of this new doctrine
on the ground.

It is for those lieutenants that Captains Michael L.
Burgoyne and Albert J. Marckwardt have written *The
Defense of Jisr al-Doreaa*. Worthy successors to E. D.
Swinton and James R. McDonough, these veterans
have reflected on their experience in Iraq and written
a guide to the tactical challenges of that conflict that is
sure to become a modern classic. One can almost hear
a lieutenant—we'll call him "Phil Connors"—appointed
to defend a bridge in Baghdad, saying plaintively, "Now,
if they had given me a job like fighting the Battle of Waterloo, or Gettysburg, or Desert Storm, I knew all about
that . . ."

After reading both these accounts of learning the hard

way, any lieutenant would be better prepared to fight wars, armed with lessons from history and with lasting principles of counterinsurgency provided by the captains and colonels of today and of years gone by.

*John A. Nagl*

John Nagl is a senior fellow at the Center for a New American Security, Washington, DC. A retired U.S. Army officer, he fought in Iraq in 2003 and 2004 and returned in 2008 for a ten-day inspection visit sponsored by Multi-National Forces Iraq. Nagl helped write *The U.S. Army/Marine Corps Counterinsurgency Field Manual* and is the author of *Learning to Eat Soup with a Knife*, both published by the University of Chicago Press.

SOLDIERS FROM 3RD PLATOON, C TROOP, 3–7 CAVALRY. BACK ROW, LEFT TO RIGHT: SGT(P) RODRIGUEZ, 2LT DE JESUS MORALES, SGT COCHRAN, SFC JOHNSON. FRONT ROW, LEFT TO RIGHT: SSG(P) WILLIAMS, SGT TRAYLOR, SGT LIESBISH, SSG SOWBY.

# THE
# DEFENSE
# OF
# JISR AL-
# DOREAA

# PREFACE

This is another type of war new in its intensity, ancient in its origins—war by guerrillas, subversives, insurgents, assassins; war by ambush instead of by combat; by infiltration, instead of aggression, seeking victory by eroding and exhausting the enemy instead of engaging him . . . it requires in those situations where we must counter it . . . a wholly different kind of force, and therefore a new and wholly different kind of military training.

—President John F. Kennedy

Remarks to the graduating class, U.S. Military Academy, 1962

The following story embodies the recollection of things done and undone in Iraq between 2003 and 2008. The advent of the War on Terror and the evolution of guerrilla tactics into a decisive type of combat in its urban and rural forms have changed the way that Western forces conduct warfare. The U.S. deployments to Iraq and Afghanistan have taught us a plethora of lessons, leading to multiple adjustments to doctrine. In the spirit of continuing that learning process, we are harking back to officer training and the simple but effective novella, *The Defence of Duffer's Drift*, which appears later in this book. Inspired by E. D. Swinton and his character, "Backsight Forethought," we've sketched a story that we believe will be of value to any young officer or small-unit leader engaged in the complexities of counterinsurgency warfare.

We hope that the pages that follow illustrate the critical fundamentals of counterinsurgency and promote the application of hard-won lessons. As the forces of liberal democracy continue to face the challenge of radical extremists, we offer this simple text as a basis for additional study and discussion of counterinsurgency tactics.

*Captain Michael L. Burgoyne*
*Captain Albert J. Marckwardt*

# ACKNOWLEDGMENTS

The lessons in this book grew out of the insights of the Soldiers, officers, and non-commissioned officers who served under me during my command in Iraq. I want especially to acknowledge Staff Sergeant Curtis Mitchell, who paid the ultimate price and who continues to inspire those who knew him. Sergeant Major Tony Broadhead and the Soldiers of Crazyhorse Troop, Third Squadron, 7th U.S. Cavalry, achieved great success; I want to thank them for the honor of serving with them, learning counterinsurgency on the job. I'm also deeply grateful to Colonel Michael Johnson, Lieutenant Colonel Christopher DeLaRosa, Lieutenant Colonel Paul Reese, Lieutenant Colonel Jeffery Broadwater, Lieutenant Colonel Antonio Aguto, Colonel William Dolan, and Colonel Terry Ferrell for their mentorship.

Colonel James Mingo at the National Training Center encouraged me to capitalize on my role as an observer controller and gave me the time and motivation I needed to put my thoughts onto paper. General Steven Salazar and Colonel Randal Dragon demonstrated that their focus on counterinsurgency fundamentals would train units more effectively, and helped inspire me to write *The Defense of Jisr al-Doreaa*.

I would also like to thank Lieutenant Colonel John Nagl, for shepherding the book along so that it could be published, and Maggie Hivnor and the great folks at University of Chicago Press, for publishing it as they have.

Additional thanks go to Mike Goldfarb, Mike Mc-Callister, and the great people at Mc Murry, for creating the book's Web site. Special thanks to Uncle Grant, for introducing me to *Duffer's Drift*.

My wife, Shelly, and son, Ulysses, have enabled the whole process and continue to support me in all my endeavors.

*Michael L. Burgoyne*

Thanks to all the Soldiers, non-commissioned officers, and lieutenants of B Troop, Third Squadron, 7th U.S. Cavalry, for truly teaching me the applied art and science of counterinsurgency during our time in Adhamiyah, Baghdad, for OIF V . . . your professionalism inspired everyone you touched, and I am honored to have witnessed your greatness. First Sergeant Farr, Sergeant First Class Lugo, Sergeant First Class Hall, Sergeant First Class Mao, and Sergeant First Class Gore, thanks for leading the troop to victory; you are the epitome of the NCO Corps.

Lieutenant Colonel Jeffery Broadwater, thanks for your leadership, mentorship, and guidance while we trained for and fought in Iraq; it was a privilege to command for you. Major Ike Sallee and Major Glen Clubb, thanks for the endless hours of debate; both of you challenged me continually and forced me to keep expanding my horizons.

Colonel Mike Johnson, Lieutenant Colonel Paul Reese, Lieutenant Colonel David Oeschger, and Lieutenant Colonel Robert Reynolds, thanks for your patience in mentoring me as a staff officer during OIF III and properly preparing me to command in combat. Major Colin Wooten, thanks for teaching me the importance of OPDs while I was a lieutenant, and influencing me to read *The Defence of Duffer's Drift*; I always followed your example while in command. Major Everret Spain, thanks for taking the time to review our work and give us feedback while you were in Iraq. Tom Ricks, thanks for reading the book and helping us in its publishing.

My parents, Albert and Gloria, and my sister, Kim, thanks for supporting me and providing stability while I went on my adventures to Iraq—never could have done it without you.

*Jim Marckwardt*

# ACRONYMS AND TERMS

| | |
|---:|:---|
| *abaya* | a loose-fitting garment, usually black, worn by Muslim women in Arabic-speaking regions. |
| ACOG | advanced combat optical gun sight |
| AIF | anti-Iraqi forces |
| AO | area of operations |
| BDA | battle damage assessment |
| BRADLEY | Bradley fighting vehicle; also M-3 or CFV |
| CLASS IV | obstacle and construction supplies |
| CO | commanding officer |
| COP | combat outpost |
| CP | command post |
| DOW | died of wounds |
| EOD | explosive ordnance disposal |
| EOF | escalation of force |
| FOB | forward operating base |
| FSO | fire support officer |
| GPS | global positioning system |
| HA | humanitarian assistance |
| HEMTT | heavy equipment–medium truck transport |
| HMMWV | highly mobile multi-wheeled vehicle |
| HVT | high-value target |
| IA | Iraqi army |
| IED | improvised explosive device |
| IP | Iraqi police |
| IR | infrared |
| ISF | Iraqi security forces |
| ISU | integrated sight unit; gunner's optic on a Bradley |

| | |
|---|---|
| JUNDEE | Iraqi soldier |
| KIA | killed in action |
| LZ | landing zone |
| MBTR | multiband intrateam radio |
| MEDEVAC | medical evacuation |
| MRE | meal ready to eat |
| NCO | non-commissioned officer |
| PVT | private |
| QRF | quick reaction force |
| REDCON | readiness condition |
| RIP | relief in place |
| ROE | rules of engagement |
| RPG | rocket-propelled grenade |
| RTO | radio telephone operator |
| SITREP | situation report |
| SOP | standing operating procedure |
| SP | start point |
| SPC | specialist |
| SQUAD-DESIGNATED MARKSMAN | soldier with additional marksmanship training and a more accurate M-16A4 rifle |
| STAND TO | to take up positions for action |
| TACTICAL SITE EXPLOITATION | evidence and intelligence collection for use in future operations and/or criminal prosecution |
| TCP | traffic control point |
| TRP | target reference point |
| USAID | United States Agency for International Development |
| VBIED | vehicle-borne improvised explosive device |
| WILCO | will comply |
| XO | executive officer |

# PROLOGUE

I had just completed the Basic Officers Course and after a brief time at home station was on my way to meet up with my unit in Kuwait as it prepared to move north into Iraq. I despise flying, so as the chartered jet lifted off from the United States I took two sleeping pills. The in-flight film was some old war movie about the French in Africa, but I couldn't pay attention; my thoughts kept drifting back to Iraq and my new platoon. At some point my racing imagination yielded to the effect of the pills, and I fell into an uncomfortable sleep. As my story unfolds you will see that I endured six harrowing dreams during the flight. In each dream I was faced with the same mission, troops, and terrain, but without cumulative knowledge of the situation. At the conclusion of each dream, I was able to develop critical lessons from my successes and failures. These lessons, the only recollections I retained between dreams, served to guide me on my next attempt. In the end these lessons produced success, and when I awoke I recalled them all in detail.

*2LT Phil Connors*

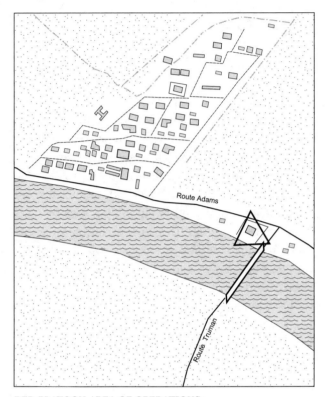

**RED PLATOON AREA OF OPERATIONS**

# THE FIRST DREAM

Thus one who excels at warfare first establishes himself in
a position where he cannot be defeated.

—Sun-tzu, *The Art of War*

Captain Brown wasted no time in rattling off the details
of my mission.

"I need you to establish a COP overwatching this pon-
toon bridge at Jisr al-Doreaa." Using the satellite imagery,
he pointed to a small line crossing a river.

"You will control your area of operations, including
the village of al-Doreaa, from your COP and prevent
anti-Iraqi forces from moving across the bridge from
the east to the west. The troop and I will continue our
operations from the FOB, so support may be a good distance from your position. I'm going to plus you up with
the mortarmen as additional dismounts and a couple of
guys from headquarters; I think you'll need some extra
manpower down there. Do you have any questions?"

Visions of Silver Stars and general officer adulation
swirled about my head. "No problem, sir!"

The commander smiled—somewhat uneasily, I
thought—and asked, "Do you need anything else for
the operation?"

I had five M-1114 armored highly mobile multi-
wheeled vehicles with .50-caliber machine guns and
MK-19 automatic grenade launchers; three M-3 Bradley
cavalry fighting vehicles with their 25-mm chain guns;

Red Platoon Task Organization

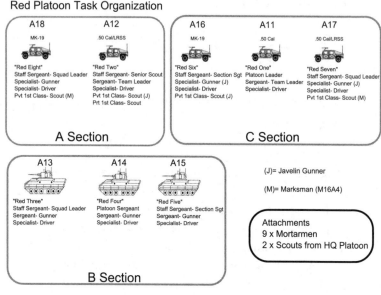

OVERVIEW OF AVAILABLE EQUIPMENT AND PERSONNEL IN
RED PLATOON

countless M-4 rifles; and a couple of M-240 machine
guns. I had thirty highly trained cavalry scouts and
NCOs. I couldn't think of anything else worth bringing. "No, sir, we're good to go."

While the platoon prepared to move, I looked over
the intelligence summaries and satellite imagery. It appeared that al-Doreaa was not particularly dangerous,
with no more than the typical IED attacks and small-
arms ambushes along major routes. But U.S. presence
in the area had been extremely limited in the last year,
so detailed recent information was largely lacking. The
surrounding population was small, about five hundred

people, and predominantly Sunni Muslim. *No major threats there*, I thought; I was almost disappointed that my first mission would be such a cakewalk.

The satellite imagery delineated my zone with a blue line that cut across the rural village and the surrounding farms. A blue triangle was placed over a small government building near the bridge that was to be my outpost. It seemed like a good spot. I grabbed my section sergeants and briefed a quick order before the pre-combat inspections. I was proud of myself for working through the troop-leading procedures just as I had learned them in school. We rehearsed the movement and occupation plan and then lined up for SP.

As we moved into zone, the rumbling of the Bradley tracks on the pavement and the hot wind blowing in my face gave me a feeling of invulnerability. I took the opportunity to observe the lay of the land from the hatch of my Bradley. Along the river, dense foliage and reeds severely restricted observations and fields of fire. Beyond the riverbanks, fields of crops stretched out to the horizon, broken only by more reeds shooting up here and there from canals that cut a chaotic web of impassible trenches into the ground. Al-Doreaa was just a cluster of mud-brick huts; only a few homes and shops boasted a sturdier concrete-and-rebar construction. As we rolled by, children who seemed eager to look at our Bradleys and trucks were quickly whisked inside by their mothers. A number of men gave us hard stares. *Go ahead: take a shot, tough guy*, I thought. I was eager to get in a fight and earn my Combat Action Badge. As I war-gamed a valiant firefight in my head, I was brought back to the task at hand by Red 2, my senior scout.

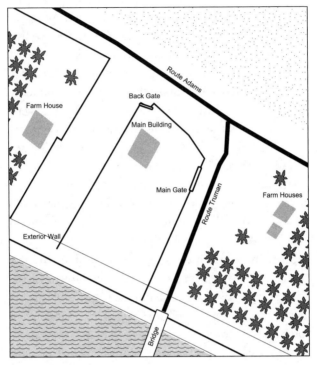

RED PLATOON'S COMBAT OUTPOST

"Red 1, Red 2; we're at the COP," the radio crackled.

"Roger. Occupy."

I dismounted the Bradley to check out our new home. A tall concrete-block wall surrounded the outpost and extended to the bank of the river. The wall had two entrances: a metal gate on its east side large enough for vehicles, and a smaller gate to the north. Inside was an unkempt yard with a small lawn. Rows of trees followed the wall's interior down to the riverbank. The south edge of the property along the water was marked with a two-foot wall. At the north end of the enclosure sat the main building. Built of concrete, with a flat roof typical of the region, it was either an old police checkpoint or former army position. It had been gutted by looters; the electrical wiring and plumbing had been torn out and graffiti covered the walls. There were three large rooms we could use for sleeping quarters, and the concrete-block construction offered good cover from small-arms fire. This would do just fine.

The sun was beginning to set across the river, and I realized we had had a long day jumping through our asses to get down here. I tried to think of my next move. My leader book from the Scout Leaders Course was full of old high-intensity conflict doctrine and check-lists. *They'd be of no use here*, I thought; *this is a new kind of war*. The old rules don't apply. The days of a dug-in tank defense were over. Besides, what kind of insurgent force would take on Bradleys and American troops armed with M-4 rifles and M-240 machine guns? I decided I would take care of my Soldiers by letting them get as much rest as possible. I called the platoon sergeant over.

"Sergeant, we'll man two Brads tonight, two men per Brad; have them overwatch the roads and the bridge. Go ahead and make the rest plan; we'll get hot tomorrow on the mission."

"Roger, sir."

The cots were set up, and the MREs came out. While my MRE beef stew was cooking in its chemical pouch, I placed my rifle in the corner and happily removed my heavy body armor. My shoulders and back ached from a long day burdened by the weight of my equipment. Sitting in the cool night air, my section sergeants and I dug into our dinners. After dessert (a bag of Skittles) we began a game of Spades on a makeshift table of cardboard MRE boxes. Red 5 and I were trouncing the platoon sergeant and Red 2 when a call came over the handheld radio.

"Red 1, this is Red 4 golf . . . I've got two locals here; I think they want to talk to you."

Throwing on my gear, I walked out to the road, where two people were standing in the headlights of the Bradley. As I got closer I could make out two men wearing "man-dresses"—"I'll never understand why they wear those things," I murmured to myself as I approached them—one tall and thin, the other relatively short. As soon as they saw me, both began frantically gesturing and babbling in Arabic. Since I couldn't understand a word they were saying, I tried to catch on by reading their body language. The stumpy man, clearly so scared he was starting to cry, kept pointing at my rifle and waving his hands, yelling, "BOOM, BOOM, BOOM." The beanpole grew angry, asking, "Mutargem? Mutargem?"

After about fifteen minutes of incomprehension, I told them to leave by using a shooing motion. When they just kept on babbling, I raised my voice, grabbed my rifle, pulled it to the low ready, and yelled, "Enough! Get out of here!" They took the hint, quickly disappearing into the shadows.

By the time I got back inside the COP, the game had broken up. Most of the guys were already asleep. I was surprised to see that many of them had moved their cots outside or onto the roof, but guessed they figured it was more comfortable to sleep outdoors, where there was a pleasant breeze. Agreeing with their assessment, I stripped off my gear, pausing for a moment to look toward the river. I could hear the water lapping at the near bank and the buzz of insects in the reeds; everything seemed peaceful. I lay down on my cot in the courtyard and, staring at the stars and imagining the glories of combat ahead, drifted off to sleep.

I awoke when my body hit the ground, debris still flying through the air. My ears were ringing; everything seemed to be moving in slow motion: dirt, rocks, sand, concrete, and ash were pelting me. I strained to focus in the dim light and slowly regained my senses. Looking toward the road, all I could see was a billowing cloud of black smoke obscuring the early morning sun. Turning, I saw that the rest of the men were as stunned as I was, most of them still half naked, staring blankly at the smoke and debris. One of the men ran to me from the gate and yelped out his contact report.

"Sir, a car . . . was hauling ass . . . drove right by us . . . and blew up next to 15 . . . it's on fire, sir, and 14's turret was damaged."

I grabbed him by the shoulders. "Calm down, man. Do we have any casualt—" I was interrupted by a blast of air and steel that threw me off my feet.

Pain shot through my arm. Looking up from the ground, I watched five more mortar rounds crash into the outpost. The men scrambled to don their body armor and seek cover, but many didn't make it, torn to pieces by the shards of metal that rang through the compound.

When the barrage stopped, I got to my feet, slung

on my armor, and ran to the gate. 15 was on fire, with 25-mm rounds cooking off in the back. The charred remains of a sedan, barely recognizable as a car frame, lay next to the Bradley. 14 was in bad shape; the sedan's engine block had impacted the gun barrel and the ISU sight, making it impossible to fire. Just as I was deciding that I would need to man the other vehicles to get some security out, I heard the chatter of machine-gun fire coming from the west side of the compound, followed by the popping of M-4s.

Inside the outpost, the platoon was firing into the southwest side of the compound. Green tracer bullets were raking the compound from the corner, and masked men were pouring through a gap in the wall where it met the water. I heard the loud crack and zing of rounds and felt chips from the wall behind me bounce off my helmet. I ducked and ran toward the cement building. The yard was filled with bodies. Blood was everywhere, and smoke from the burning vehicles by the gate made it hard to breathe. Chased by a hail of AK-47 fire, I dove through the front doorway.

Inside, the medic was working on five men; one was missing a leg. I grabbed ahold of the manpack we had been using for radio checks and called for help. I could only pray that the antenna wire hadn't been cut in the attack.

"Any station this net, any station this net, this is Red 1. We're under attack! We're under attack!"

An unintelligible blast of squelch was all that came back across. I hoped the message got through, but I couldn't be sure. I counted ten men left inside the building, some wounded, all shooting from the windows and doors.

We were beginning to run low on ammunition when the shooting suddenly stopped, and the AIF began to break contact and move back, out of the compound. I heard the steady *whomp-whomp-whomp* of the Apache helicopters before I saw them come into view, circling the compound. The medic began working on my arm. We had lost fifteen men KIA, one man DOW, and four seriously wounded. We lost two Bradleys, and most of our other vehicles were damaged.

While I waited for the MEDEVAC, I tried to figure out where I had gone so terribly wrong.

1. Security is the number-one priority. Units must maintain 360-degree security no matter what the situation.
2. The fundamentals still apply. Counterinsurgency operations and low-intensity conflict do not negate the value of systems time tested in countless conflicts. When establishing an outpost, it is critical to employ the fundamentals of defense, the seven steps of engagement area development, and the priorities of work.

As the pain of my injury burned these lessons into my memory, I found myself somehow drifting into another dream.

# THE SECOND DREAM

Never pick a fight with people who buy ink by the barrel.

—Old press adage

Adapt yourself to the things among which your lot has been cast and love sincerely the fellow creatures with whom destiny has ordained that you shall live.

—Marcus Aurelius, *The Meditations*

I again found myself in the commander's room, receiving my brief. I listened intently, determined to learn from the mistakes I'd made in the last dream. As before, I issued a warning order, giving my Soldiers the down-and-dirty information they needed to prepare for the mission, and ran through my pre-combat inspections. This time, however, I reviewed the leader book I had created in my Basic Course. I thumbed through the laminated pages to find the defensive priorities of work. They were based on seven steps of engagement area development.

1.  Identify all likely enemy avenues of approach.
2.  Determine the likely enemy scheme of maneuver.
3.  Determine where to kill the enemy.
4.  Plan and integrate obstacle/engineer effort.
5.  Emplace weapons systems.

6. Plan and integrate indirect fires.
7. Rehearse.

At first I was a little confused at how my SOP would work; I mean, it was designed for a linear armor defense against the Soviet horde. But as I looked over my notes, I found that some points in the book did apply to my current problem; they just needed to be adjusted to our particular mission and terrain.

For example, "enemy effects" would mean mortar attacks rather than attacks by air, field artillery, or chemicals, since the insurgents didn't have those capabilities. The "engineers and obstacles" listed in the book made no sense when I pictured the Maginot line, but as I looked at the satellite imagery I realized that I would need obstacle material to reinforce the outpost and our positions around it. Obstacle material would also be useful for slowing down any VBIEDs trying to get to our Bradleys. I made sure to focus not just on battle positions or vehicle fighting positions but also on our dismounted positions; these would work as a perimeter defense. I knew that the rules of engagement limited my indirect fire assets. Firing artillery would be a real hassle with all the levels of approval required up the chain of command. Since I couldn't expect to get 155-mm artillery support without the division commander signing off, I focused instead on how I could use more readily available support from the air.

Armed with this analysis, I returned to the commander with a list of requests. After some discussion and a couple of calls to Squadron, I managed to get one HEMTT 10-ton cargo truck with 5,000 sandbags, 4

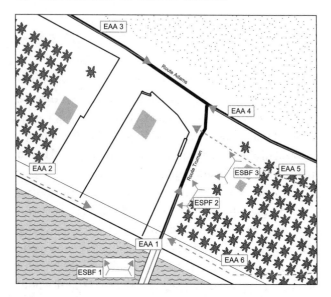

RED PLATOON'S ENEMY SITUATION TEMPLATE USED TO
SHOW POSSIBLE ENEMY COURSES OF ACTION. INCLUDES
ENEMY AVENUES OF APPROACH 1–6 AND ENEMY SUPPORT-BY-
FIRE POSITIONS 1–3.

short concrete jersey barriers, and 100 rolls of concertina wire. I learned that attack aviation was set for troops
in contact and would be on a fifteen-minute string if we
needed them. The commander also recommended that
I pass along any graphics to the troop executive officer
to coordinate with the pilots.

With my trusty SOP and a HEMTT full of class IV, I
left the gate, bound for the outpost with the same ample
forces I had in my first dream. As soon as we arrived
at the outpost, I reached into my bag, pulled out my

leader book, and began ticking off the priorities of work. Overall the terrain was going to favor the enemy: high-speed paved roads allowed quick access to the COP, the riverbank provided a great obstacle behind which he could engage us, and the farms and river foliage enabled concealed approaches toward our position. I sketched out the likely enemy avenues of approach. Route Adams moved from the southeast to the northwest, passing just north of the outpost, while Route Truman crossed the bridge, intersecting Route Adams at the corner of the outpost. I identified some dismounted approaches using the cover from the dense foliage by the river. I also got down on the ground and determined that the most likely way for AIF to attack the outpost would be a dismounted assault along the river or a VBIED traveling down Route Adams or Truman. They would need a support-by-fire position, from which they could keep our heads down while they crossed the road and breached the wall; they could even establish their position on the far side of the river.

After reviewing these enemy options, I created our platoon direct-fire plan. I figured that the best place to kill the bad guys would be as they crossed Routes Adams or Truman, or in the obstacles we could set up. I showed the platoon sergeant where these obstacles would go: We'd reinforce the outer wall with concertina wire, pulling it all the way down to the river. To fix the enemy for our direct fires, we'd also need wire outside the perimeter, on the other side of the roads and the canal to the north. The cement barricades would be placed at the intersection and along the avenues of approach. Finally, we would use sandbags to reinforce the

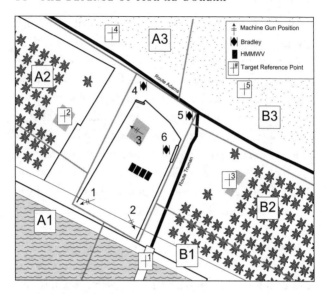

RED PLATOON'S DIRECT FIRE PLAN, INCLUDING FRIENDLY
POSITIONS 1–6, TARGET REFERENCE POINTS 1–5, AND
QUADRANTS A1, A2, A3, B1, B2, AND B3.

building and cover the windows as well as build bunkers
for our machine-gun positions.

While the obstacles were being put in place, I made
sure we manned our Bradleys, pulling security the entire
time. I then directed the establishment of our defensive
positions. Two dug-in and sandbagged bunkers would
cover the southern approaches as well as the opposite
side of the river. One machine gun on the roof would
cover the northwest. Two Bradleys would sit on the main
road, while another Bradley would simultaneously block
the main gate and cover the eastern approaches. The

commo sergeant ran wire to all the positions and established a command and control node in the main building, so that we had both FM radio and wire communication between all my elements.

As the last light faded quickly into the west, I went out one last time to check our defenses from the enemy's perspective. They seemed pretty imposing. As I walked around the outpost, I radioed to confirm that we had overlapping fires throughout the perimeter. The platoon sergeant kept the men working all night filling sandbags and improving our force protection measures; their guard rotation was demanding but workable.

I finally went inside the main building and set up my cot. The air within was still hot from the scorching day and rank with the sweat of sleeping Soldiers. I felt a moment of self-pity knowing I, too, would be sweating all night, but our stuffy quarters offered the best protection from enemy fire. Confident that I had done what I could to establish a strong defense and knowing that we would continue to improve through the night and coming days, I went to sleep.

Stand To was at 0530 hours; by then the entire platoon was up, manning the perimeter. I remembered my grizzly NCO instructor at ROTC telling me, "The Indians attack at dawn . . . that's why we do Stand To." Well, by 0600 they hadn't attacked, so I indulged in a shave and a quick MRE breakfast. (In my haste, I grabbed a thick, brown plastic bag and tore it open, only to find I'd chosen the burrito meal, so I had to discard the main meal and pick through the rest, wolfing down a pound cake along with some crackers with jalapeno cheese.)

I trooped the line, inspecting each position, quizzing

the Soldiers on their sectors and their target reference points. Each Soldier would need to know what he was responsible for observing. When I reached the Bradleys, one of the vehicle commanders called out to me.

"Hey sir, when can we shoot at vehicles? We've been letting 'em roll by so far."

Since I thought I'd made my guidance clear during the initial occupation the night before, this was more than a little frustrating. I was gravely concerned that a VBIED might get through the perimeter. "Look, nothing gets through here. Nothing. Just turn them around, and if they don't stop, *engage them*. Remember, those VBIEDs are deadly!"

"Roger, sir."

All that day, the men cut down reeds and foliage to clear fields of fire, set up bunkers, and finished reinforcing the building. Darkness fell, and the guard shifts flowed through the night. Enveloped by the stagnant air of the concrete building, I slept, my rest interrupted only a few times by shots from the Bradley as they turned back cars trying to move down Route Adams or across the bridge. When morning brought another uneventful Stand To, I found myself feeling more and more confident.

"I guess the AIF know who not to mess with . . . and I thought this would be a fight down here," I boasted to the platoon sergeant.

While I was walking the line about 0700, I heard a shot that I thought was the Bradleys again, except that it sounded louder and more distant . . . then the screaming started.

"MEDIC! MEDIC!"

Running toward the cries near the center of the outpost, I was startled by a burst from the M-240 on the roof. As I reached the building, I found our medic near its wall, staring at the body of one of my privates, who seemed to be sleeping or unconscious—until I noticed a small hole just below his ear, and blood pooling on the opposite side of his Kevlar. The medic just knelt beside him, his lips moving in a silent prayer. Everyone inside the house came running out, shocked at the sight of their friend. The platoon sergeant covered his body with a poncho liner.

"Man your positions!" he growled. They scattered. I grabbed the closest man to ask what had happened.

"He was going up on the roof for his shift when he got hit."

Hoping to get a handle on the situation, I began, carefully, to climb up to the roof. My heart was thumping loudly in my ears as I made my way up. When I reached the top, I dove into the bunker, happy to be alive, and asked the men there what they were shooting at. They said they thought the fatal shot had come from TRP 2, a farmhouse about 250 meters away to the northwest. That made little sense to me, because my Soldier's wound suggested that the shot had come from the southeast. But I knew that snipers were dangerous, and I wasn't about to let my Soldier die for nothing. *Better be sure*, I thought. I called over the net to the other positions.

"Engage all possible sniper locations!"

Red 2 came back: "Sir, including the farmhouses?"

"Yep, *all* possible sniper hide sites!"

The roar of the machine guns echoed across the farmland as 7.62 rounds zipped through the flimsy farmhouses and skipped through the surrounding fields in a "mad minute" that reminded me of the Arnold Schwarzenegger movie *Predator*.

When I was satisfied, I radioed a ceasefire. I spoke to the machine gunner again. "So what else did you see?" He replied that he had seen an Iraqi run out of the farmhouse toward town, but that when his buddy got shot, he had dropped his gun to try to help him. *There was no one out to cut that guy off, so I guess he got away . . . or maybe we were lucky and got him in one of the houses*, I thought.

Screams and cries interrupted me again—female, Iraqi screams, coming from the farmhouse to the east. I slid down the ladder to the ground and organized a five-man patrol to go to the farmhouse, bringing the medic just in case we had casualties. As we pushed out the main gate, I saw a young woman clutching a child, about five or six years old, in her arms. His left arm was a shredded stump from the elbow down; his chest was mangled and drenched in blood, with bits of shattered bone protruding from gaping exit wounds caused by 7.62 bullets. Her cries were not really cries—that word doesn't do them justice—they were animal noises, guttural and piercing, filled with anguish and disbelief.

The medic tried to examine the child—why, I'm not sure; he was so clearly dead. The distraught mother reared away from the medic, losing her grip on the boy, who tumbled out of her arms. Screaming, flailing, and striking out at the medic with her fists, she finally collapsed next to her son's corpse.

In the house, we discovered her husband, two daughters, and an old woman, all shredded by our machine-gun fire. No rifles, no shell casings, no sign of the AIF anywhere. I returned to the woman and tried to speak to her, but she could only weep. As I was trying to decipher her few words of Arabic, a flurry of shots rang out from the road, followed by screeching tires and a loud crash.

I ran toward the street with my patrol, hearing the radio squawk, "This is Red 5; engaged one civilian vehicle trying to run the position." As we approached the vehicle, a small, blue, four-door Volkswagen Brazil with a hatchback, we saw a man slumped over in the driver seat, his head canoed by a 5.56 round through the skull. Keeping a lookout for signs of explosives, we cautiously crept up to the passenger side of the car. In the seat a middle-aged man in a business suit was moaning and gripping his left arm, which was bleeding profusely. We pulled him from the car so that the medic could began working on him, just as one of my Soldiers brought me the dead driver's wallet. It contained several identification cards. One, printed in English and Arabic, said:

MEMBER, PROVINCIAL COUNCIL.

At this point my day really started to get difficult.

"Red 1, this is Red 2; I've got a group of people coming from town, and some of them have cameras. I think they may be media."

Just what I needed: media at this mess. When I met them at the barricades, their cameras were already rolling. I recognized a cable television news crew with a woman I had seen on TV before, reporting from Africa or some other hot spot. I introduced myself, and the questions started.

"What happened here, Lieutenant?"

"Look, I have no time for this right now; I'm in the middle of a situation!" I was not going to be intimidated by a journalist.

"Who was shot here today? Was someone shot?"

"Yes, ma'am, we have been in a firefight with some enemy snipers today." She and her crew moved to the peppered vehicle and, to my surprise, began speaking to the wounded passenger in fluent Arabic. She was able to get the full story from him. She related to me that the man was the assistant to a provincial council member—the dead man; they had been driving to Baghdad and had come upon the checkpoint, where they were engaged without warning.

"Do you have signs to warn people of an approaching checkpoint?" She asked.

"No."

"What about warning shots—were they fired?"

"No, but I can tell you that I have taken every measure to protect my Soldiers. These men could have been suicide bombers. These men should have been more careful."

At this point the blood-soaked woman came onto the road and screamed at the cameras. After another conversation in Arabic, the news crew moved to the farmhouse. I followed sheepishly behind.

"What about *this*?! What did *these* people do?" The reporter was almost weeping herself as she asked.

"I don't know," I stammered. "We thought they might be snipers, so we engaged the house. I lost a Soldier today, but I guess no one cares! This mission is hopeless! I hate this place as much as anyone else."

When the reporter did her standup, it was with the

perforated car behind her. She started by saying, "Out-of-control U.S. forces have yet again used unrestrained force in Iraq, and the Iraqis continue to pay the price. This time a provincial council member is dead, his assistant wounded when negotiating one of the most dangerous things in Iraq . . . a U.S. checkpoint. At nearly the same time a family is devastated by U.S. machine-gun fire. All while the leader of U.S. forces on the scene acts without conscience or prudence."

While I was imagining how this would look on my officer evaluation report, a guy at the gate called me.

"Hey sir, CO wants you on the radio, and I think he's pissed!"

The CO was already on the road; I could tell from the sound over the hand mike.

"Red 1, this is Apache 6; I am on my way down there now! Why haven't you been up on the net?!"

"Roger, sir, I've had some problems down here."

"Yeah, roger! Look, guy, just sit tight; I'm coming into your zone now . . ." and he cut off.

A loud boom shook the air around the outpost. The machine gun position on the roof yelled out.

"Looks like a convoy just hit an IED to the northwest!"

Frantically I called over the net "Apache 6, this is Red 1 . . . Apache 6, this is Red 1, over."

Finally, he came back across. "Red 1, this is Apache 6. You are done! Sit tight. You are relieved as soon as I get to your position."

As I sunk down in my chair by the radio awaiting my relief for cause, I thought about what I had done wrong this time. My defense of the outpost had seemed perfect.

I had checked every block and followed doctrine, but I still blew it! Tears began to run down my cheeks, first for my dead Soldier and then for the civilians we had killed. "How was I supposed to know about this stuff? What am I supposed to do?" Eventually, I arrived at the following lessons:

3. You can't fulfill the mission from inside a fortified position. Providing good security is a must, but having a fortress mentality without patrolling outside leaves you open to attack.

4. Be prepared for how the enemy will adapt to your actions. The enemy will change his strategy based on your capabilities.

5. Employ countersniper measures. Countersniper considerations must be taken into account when establishing an outpost. Sniper screens, countersniper teams, and countersniper battle drills must be implemented.

6. Briefing and enforcing rules of engagement are critical to mission accomplishment. Escalation of force and rules of engagement protect Soldiers by allowing them to engage quickly when it's necessary and to avoid wounding or killing innocent civilians.

7. Soldiers and leaders must be prepared to speak to the media. The media can help or hinder your mission both locally and globally. Use the media to highlight your victories and be prepared to answer tough questions about your actions.

Just then the CO pulled up and began to yell, his profanity blending into colors and a swirling mix of sounds as I drifted off into my third dream, armed with five new lessons.

# THE THIRD DREAM

It is never wise to let the enemy get used to a certain form of warfare; it is necessary to vary constantly the places, the hours, and the forms of operations.

—Ernesto "Che" Guevara, *Guerrilla Warfare* (1961)

Once again I received my orders and conducted my preparation, intent on accomplishing my mission. This time I carefully reread my escalation of force and rules of engagement, noting the principles outlined in the SOP:

1. Soldiers always have the right to defend themselves.
2. If the situation allows, use graduated force, including nonlethal means, before using lethal force.
3. You don't have to go through all the steps if deadly force is deemed necessary.

The graduated response followed some simple and easy-to-remember steps, which I briefed my Soldiers on before leaving the FOB.

- Shout—A verbal warning or gesture
- Show—Display your weapon and intent to use it

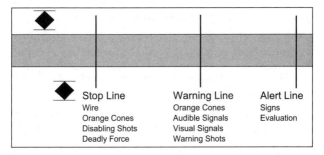

TRAFFIC CONTROL POINT DIAGRAM FROM 2LT CONNORS'S
STANDING OPERATING PROCEDURES

- Shove—Physically detain or restrain
- Shoot—Warning shot first, then shots to kill

Thinking about how I could apply the ROE to my Bradley positions on the road, I went back to the SOP and found the traffic-control-point diagram. Based on the diagram, I made a quick supply list for the XO, including laser pointers, spotlights, warning signs, and orange cones, which he was able to issue to me just before it was time to leave.

Movement to the outpost was uneventful. I established my defense as I had before, meticulously going through my priorities of work. The Soldiers worked to fortify their positions, and the guard roster was implemented. I added a few more defensive measures to protect the outpost from sniper activity. We draped camouflage netting over all our positions, including the Bradley turrets. I had my squad designated marksman establish a countersniper position on the roof of the outpost using his upgraded M-16A4 with ACOG optic. I also reviewed all our positions and determined the most likely sniper hide sites; those sites were then briefed to the Soldiers on duty and added to the range cards for constant observation.

Out front on the route, I inspected our new TCP for compliance with rules of engagement. Red 5 back-briefed me on his EOF steps.

"Sir, out around 350 meters, I've got the signs set up. Not sure exactly what they say, but I think they will let the Hajis know there is a checkpoint ahead. After that, we have an orange cone for the warning line with a yellow flag and yellow chem light. If they are still moving fast, we have the spotlights you gave us and the laser pointers."

He shined the green laser down the street. It was surprisingly visible, even in the early dusk. "At that point, sir, if they're still coming, they will hit the jersey barriers, and we will fire warning shots, followed by shots to disable. And if they hit this cone"—he pointed to the orange cone topped by a red flag and chem light—"we will take them out."

"Remember, Sergeant: you need to determine hostile intent; it's not just about the steps," I reminded him. "If you determine a VBIED is coming at your alert line, you've got to engage. But at the same time, if a school bus full of nuns is failing to stop, don't vaporize it with the 25."

"Roger, sir, I briefed my guys. Follow the steps and hostile intent. Nothing to worry about here, sir, we'll pass it on to the next shifts as they come on."

Finally, I developed a dismounted patrol schedule

from the outpost to clear potential sniper positions and prevent IEDs from being emplaced on our route. The patrols would leave every four hours and would rotate between squads. To simplify the operation, I gave the patrols the same detailed route and instructions. They would first move north and check the road for IEDs, and next move through the south side of the village, then check for possible sniper sites on the east side of the outpost. *There won't be any sniper or IED activity on my watch*, I thought. The platoon sergeant adjusted the guard roster, and at nightfall the patrols began. As I drifted off to sleep, I was confident that my well-fortified position and new patrol scheme would, this time, succeed.

The next day the RTO briefed me on the night's activities. Apparently one patrol at 0200 had come up on three personnel by the road and then lost contact with them as they ran into the town. On the side of the road they had found a shovel and a small hole.

"That's one IED that won't be going off today!" I boasted.

All the more sure I was on the right track now, I decided to lead from the front and go out with my Soldiers on the next patrol. At 0900 we moved out on my route and traversed the west side of the outpost, first moving at 5-meter intervals. My 40-pound vest pulled on my shoulders. I was proud of my kit: I had two large ammo pouches in the front with six 30-round magazines, a couple of frag grenades in small pouches, a large first-aid pouch on my left side with a new Israeli bandage, a civilian GPS on my left shoulder, and a big silver trident knife on my right hip. I kept my right shoulder clear so

I could easily bring my M-4 rifle to bear on any insurgents. My rifle was covered in accessories: a PEQ-15 laser sight, ACOG sight, and a sure-fire flashlight. As the sweat began to pour down my neck, I was thankful to be wearing the new, lighter ACH Kevlar helmet with its more comfortable pads.

I was moving delicately through the reeds when we came upon the farmhouse to the west of the outpost: a two-story, concrete, framed house with brick and mortar walls. Its windows were either broken or missing, and its stucco was only sporadically present, most of it chipped off and worn by time.

An old Iraqi man was standing out front, his eyelids a wrinkled mass of skin swollen nearly shut by the sun; his weathered face and gnarled hands gave further evidence he was no stranger to working outdoors. As we approached the house, I saw a small girl, peering out from one of the lower windows, being whisked away by the black form of a woman in a full *abaya*.

Making sure to keep my right hand on my weapon, I walked up and waved to the man; I remembered from ROTC that hand and arm signals should be done with your nonfiring hand.

"Good morning, how are you?" I cheerfully asked.

He smiled and nodded.

"Have you seen any terrorists?" He continued to smile and nod.

I looked back at my RTO, and he gave me a shrug. Then the old man took me by the hand and, babbling something in Arabic, pulled me toward the side of his house to a hole in the ground. I was ecstatic, thinking, *finally a cache site: the commander will be happy about*

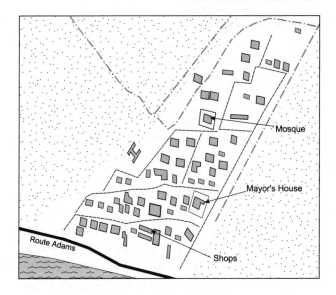

THE TOWN OF AL-DOREAA

*this!* But once I looked inside, I saw some kind of ir-
rigation pump in a sad state of disrepair. The old man
looked at me and clapped his hands together, sliding
them apart over and over—signaling, I think, that the
pump was broken.

"Sorry, can't help with that, sir; but do you know
where the bad guys are?"

He just gazed at me with an empty stare.

"Well, thanks for your time. Let us know if you see
anything." I was running out of patience. We skirted
the main road, diligently looking for signs of IED em-
placers, and then moved into the village. The day was
beginning to heat up, and I could smell the goats and

sheep in nearby pens along with the stench of raw sewage draining into shallow trenches on either side of the small dirt road. Most of the buildings were mud brick with thatch roofs, many augmented with random pieces of tin , plastic, and other building materials. People moved between the houses, apparently paying no attention to us; but as we passed a small shop, a couple of young guys, about sixteen or seventeen years old, gave us a hard look.

As we made our way toward our turn back south, two men came out of the courtyard of one of the nicer homes in the town. One was wearing a flowing white robe and a white headdress; the other was wearing gray slacks and a white shirt. They approached our patrol with smiles on their faces, then grasped my hand eagerly, shaking it, and saying something in Arabic.

"Good morning, how are you gentlemen. I'm Lieutenant Connors. I am here to help."

They looked at me and blurted something in Arabic—I had no idea what it meant. Mindful of snipers, I gestured to them to move back inside the courtyard. Once there, they both produced identification. One card, in Arabic, was of no help, but the other said:

MAYOR AL DOREAA TOWN

"Mayor? Mayor?" I nodded, pointing at him.

He smiled and yelped, "Naam, naam."

I looked at the other man and shrugged my shoulders sheepishly. "No Arabic." He looked about and then pointed skyward behind me. I saw the minaret of the village mosque.

"Oh, you're the imam?" I said.

He nodded and smiled. At this point the mayor whis-

pered to me, again in Arabic, so all I could do was nod.
He began making hand gestures that I couldn't make out.
I knew these men had something important to tell me,
but this was hopeless. After about ten minutes they grew
as frustrated as I was with our game of charades.

"I must be going. It has been nice speaking with you
gentlemen." The mayor and the imam watched us walk
off. As we left the village, the afternoon call to prayer
echoed across the town from the minaret.

At the end of our patrol I was happy to drop my sweat-
stained gear onto the outpost floor. Although the inside
of the outpost was hotter than it was outdoors, I insisted
that all personnel sleep under cover and remove their
gear only when inside. It was worth breathing that stagnant air to get out of the body armor. I lay on my cot,
reviewing the day and wondering what the men in the
village had wanted to say to me.

That evening, patrols continued every four hours
along my designated route until, after twenty-four hours
of no IEDs, it appeared that I had cracked the code on
controlling the zone. As I walked the line before bed, I
was impressed with our positions; I saw range cards at
every post, hardened with sandbags and covered with
camo netting. The Bradley positions looked great, and
the TCPs were well marked with chem lights. As I approached the first Bradley, I had the opportunity to observe the men go through the procedures on a civilian
vehicle. The vehicle approached and then slowed after
passing the sign. The Bradley commander flashed his
laser at the windshield, and the vehicle stopped and
turned around, without a shot fired. Thinking that perhaps counterinsurgency wasn't so hard after all, I went

back to my rack and dozed off, with happy visions of quick promotions in my future.

I was getting ready for Stand To the following morning when I heard an explosion in the distance, followed by bursts of automatic fire. Over the radio I heard Red 6 come across: "CONTACT! CONTACT!" with the *b-r-r-r-a-p* of machine-gun fire and the pop of M-4s in the background.

I told the platoon sergeant to replace the Bradleys on the TCPs with HMMWVs to maintain security while I reacted to the contact. I was going to help my guys. I climbed up into one of the Brads and yelled to Red 3 to prepare to move. Luckily the Bradleys were already REDCON 1 for Stand To, so we were moving in less than thirty seconds. As we weaved through the jersey barriers, the firing ceased.

"Red 6, this is Red 1!" I yelled into the mike. "Red 6, this is Red 1!"

No response.

We saw black smoke coming from the south side of the town and rushed to the site. As we entered the village, I saw men in black ski masks fleeing north with AKs and an RPK machine gun. I slewed the turret right and yelled.

"Troops right!"

The gunner hollered back, "Got 'em!"

"Fire!"

The coax machine gun coughed out a burst of 7.62; one of the men tumbled end over end like a rag doll as the bullets ripped through his torso. Red 3 was scanning to the west, and I was pulled away from the contact by his voice over the radio.

"Red 1, Red 3. I've got friendlies on the ground to our front; I think we have some wounded."

The insurgents grabbed their bloody comrade and disappeared behind a mud wall. I scanned back left and saw what Red 3 was talking about. Lying in the middle of the street were nine Soldiers, two of them writhing in the dirt, clutching at their wounds. Deciding the insurgents would have to wait, I moved to help my men. Red 3 called the platoon sergeant, and soon our medic was on the way in another convoy, along with air support for troops in contact.

The bodies of my nine men lay strewn about in pools of blood and stained brown earth. Judging by the scorch marks on the ground, an RPG had struck the patrol first. The shell casings lying all around made it clear that they had been attacked from multiple directions, ambushed in a spot where they had nowhere to go, between a mud-brick wall and a set of shops—the same shops where I had seen those two teenagers staring me down. I shuddered for a moment in selfish relief, thinking *this could have been me*. I had walked down this same road not twelve hours ago. That's when it hit me. Those same kids had seen all the patrols come by, every four hours, for the last day and a half.

I was jerked back to the task at hand by the screams of the wounded men and the hammering beat of Apache helicopters coming onto the scene. As I treated the wounded and listened to their cries, the following lessons formed in my brain, built upon the anguish of my failure:

8.  Do not set patterns. Vary routes, times, and tactics to avoid being targeted by the enemy.

9. Language skills are critical for gaining information on the enemy and coordinating with host-nation allies.

Engulfed by a swirling cloud of dust as the MEDEVAC bird was touching down, I felt the day slip away into another dream.

# THE FOURTH DREAM

It is only undisciplined troops who make the people their enemies and who, like the fish out of its native element, cannot live.

—Mao Tse-tung, *On Guerrilla Warfare* (1937)

In the main, however, we sought to carry out operations in a way that minimized the chances of creating more enemies than we captured or killed. The idea was to try to end each day with fewer enemies than we had when it started.

—General David H. Petraeus, "Learning Counterinsurgency: Observations from Soldiering in Iraq" (2006)

Mission preparation went much the same as it had before, except for a new request I made to the commander for two Iraqi interpreters. These he was able to provide, along with a short list of Arabic phrases that all Soldiers should learn and keep with them. After completing my mission brief and ROE brief I left the FOB with my EOF kit, my defensive barrier material, and the two contracted interpreters, once again confident in my ability to accomplish my mission.

Occupation of the outpost went like clockwork. To make our patrols less vulnerable to attack, I gave the men named areas of interest to observe but varied the SP times, and told them to alter their routes and directions of travel. To break up the patterns and appearance of our missions, I also shifted to setting observation post positions for short periods while on patrol. Finally, I assigned an interpreter to each patrol so they could talk to the locals.

The next morning I awoke and inspected the defenses after Stand To. When I arrived back at the main building I noticed the two interpreters. One man was still asleep from night patrols, but the other, who had a scruffy, not-quite bearded face, had just finished dressing. He wore desert-pattern fatigues and Iraqi-style body armor with a bulky square plate, a black bandanna on his head, and fingerless weight-lifting gloves. Dark sunglasses hid his identity. He introduced himself in a heavy accent.

"My name is Nasir, sir; I will be your interpreter."

"Great, Nasir; it's good to be working with you. We'll be talking to the locals today to try to get some intel on the insurgents in the area."

When I asked Nasir where he was from, he told me al-Doreaa. I briefed him thoroughly on our mission; I wanted him to understand exactly what we were doing so that he could help communicate my message to the local populace. Next I gave him a quick tour of our compound and told him to meet back up with us after lunch to conduct our mission. I was excited about having an interpreter, especially a local with personal knowledge of the area. I felt certain that he would help us gain crucial intelligence from his community.

That afternoon we moved out on patrol, exiting through the main gate. We weaved our way through the reeds northwest of the outpost, toward al-Doreaa. As we patrolled down the dusty streets, Nasir exchanged pleasantries with the townspeople and waved to those shopping at the small stores. We began rounding a street corner to head south, back toward the river, when we were met by two men—one in a pair of slacks and a white shirt, the other wearing a long white robe and headdress.

"Salaam 'aleikum." I reached to shake their hands.

The man in the robe shook my hand demurely and smiled. The man in the slacks shook my hand and smiled widely, chanting, "Ahlan wa sahlan!" To my great surprise, he leaned forward and kissed my cheek. As he swung his head around to get the other side of my face, I pulled back in revulsion.

"*Whoa!*"

While the man stared, clearly shocked by my actions, Nasir quickly whispered to me, "Sir, sir: this is common in our culture; men kiss each others' cheeks."

He spoke to the man in Arabic and then turned to me. "Sir, I told him you meant no disrespect. He is Mr. Hussein, the mayor of the village and a council member for the Qada. The other man is the town imam. Mr. Hussein has invited you into his home . . . this one right here." He pointed to a concrete framed house with a high mud-brick wall around the perimeter.

"Okay, absolutely! Let's see if he knows where the terrorists are!"

We entered a courtyard and found a small green lawn and a modest but well-kept home with a narrow porch. A Kia minivan was parked under an awning at the side of the home. We followed the men inside to a large anteroom furnished with a giant rug and several pillows. The walls were plastered with posters of beheaded men and angry-looking guys in turbans. I asked Nasir who they were.

"This one here," he pointed to one of the headless men, "is Husayn Ibn Ali, the martyr of the Shia sect of Islam. And here, this is Muktada al-Sadr; he is a very powerful Shia cleric."

I wondered if that information was worth remembering.

In the corner of the room stood a woman, covered completely in black. I approached her, trying to acknowledge her presence with a *salaam 'aleikum* and a hearty handshake. But as I reached to shake her hand, she pulled away. My interpreter immediately stepped between us, stammering, "You are dishonoring their women! You cannot speak directly to them." Mr. Hussein hastily ushered the woman out of the room and turned back to me with a look of disbelief. He regained his composure, motioned for us to sit, and yelled back into the house, "Chai! Chai!"

I told the patrol to stay outside—except for a couple of guys to watch my back—and plopped myself down on a pillow. My cumbersome gear made sitting difficult, so I kicked my legs out in front of me in an L with my back against the wall. I wanted to remove my helmet, but since my radio headset was attached to it, I kept it on. Nasir sat down next to me and crossed his legs underneath him. The mayor and the imam sat down across from us. Eyeing me sternly, the imam spoke to Nasir.

Nasir looked somewhat cowed as he leaned toward me. "Sir, you mustn't put the soles of your feet toward an Iraqi: this is insulting."

*Sure*, I thought, *but they weren't wearing 40 pounds of gear*. I shot the imam a sarcastic smile and, with some difficulty, crossed my legs.

I was about to ask where the terrorists were when a boy came into the room with a tray of small glasses. Surprised that we would be doing shots of whiskey this early in the day, I hesitantly took one of the glasses he offered. It was extremely hot and I nearly burned my fingers. I watched as Nasir stirred his glass with a diminutive spoon and then sipped on the beverage. I leaned toward him and asked, "What is this stuff? Don't they realize it's like 100 degrees outside?"

Nasir looked confused. "Sir, this is chai. It is what Iraqis drink."

I stirred the liquid, surprised by the massive mound of sugar in the bottom of the glass. I have never really liked sweets. I shrugged and took a swig, burning my tongue. I put the glass down.

The mayor looked concerned. "You don't like the chai?"

"No, no, it's too hot outside for chai," I said.

He frowned. "What is your name? Where are you from?"

"My name is Lieutenant Connors. I'm here to provide security." I wasn't about to tell him anything about myself.

"Very good, then. I have lived here my whole life. I have two daughters and a young son."

"That's fascinating, but I only need to know about the insurgents in the area. Who is planting the IEDs?"

Nasir looked concerned as he listened to me and then translated my words.

This caused another flurry of Arabic between the two men and Nasir. Once again Nasir leaned toward me and whispered.

"Sir, our way is to speak first together as men so we know about the person we are dealing with. After this, then we speak about business. How can he trust you if you will not speak with him as a person and not just a Soldier?"

I was pondering this pearl of wisdom when I noticed that the boy was bringing in some food on a large platter.

"We were just to have lunch. You will be our guests," the mayor said with a smile.

On the broad tin platter I was more than a little surprised to see half a sheep's head staring back at me with what was left of its boiled eyeball. This unappetizing apparition was surrounded by rice, flatbread, and some kind of broth. Nasir and the two men reached in and began grabbing pieces of meat from the cheek of the sheep and mixing it with the rice and bread. As I watched their fingers going from the plate to their mouths, the animal-like slurping and sucking sounds made me a little queasy. Disgusted, I tried to hold off on eating by asking a question.

"So how is the town? Do you need anything here?" The mayor looked up and grinned, food still in his teeth.

"You Americans have been here for years now. It's promise after promise. I need many things . . . clean water, power that stays on, a medical clinic with supplies. But I know you will not give me any of these things. My own daughter has been very sick for a week and we cannot treat her because there is no clinic. Let us just eat so you will not have to lie to me with promises."

While the mayor was speaking, I realized that I might

need to take some notes from this meeting. I managed with some difficulty to retrieve my notebook from my cargo pocket and locate paper and pencil.

"Sir, you must eat. They will be offended."

I was not about to consume a sheep head, so I reached for some bread and rice instead.

The imam grimaced and, in a whining exclamation, stood up and pointed.

Nasir tried to translate. "Sir, he is offended. He asks why you know nothing of their culture. You eat with your offensive hand, disrespect them with the soles of your feet, and assault their women."

The imam yelled something at the mayor and stomped out of the room. The mayor sat and looked at me from across the floor.

I said to him, "Perhaps it's best that we go."

"Perhaps." With that, he ushered us out of the room and to the gate.

I realized I had made no progress at this meeting, despite my interpreter. It seemed that no matter what I did, I infuriated the Iraqis—they seemed predisposed to be hostile, so easily offended by the smallest mistakes and the most normal behavior. Nevertheless, I was resolving to prepare more thoroughly for the next meeting with them when I heard the sound of small-arms fire in the distance near the outpost.

The radio crackled: "Contact, sniper TRP 2! OP 3, engaging!"

We double-timed it back toward the outpost.

"OP 5, contact dismounts; OP 6, they're coming your way."

"I've got 'em."

The sound of 25-mm fire ripped through the air, followed by the thuds of the high-explosive rounds.

"This is Red 1, SITREP!" I yelled into the radio.

The firing abated as we approached the outpost.

"Red 1, Red 4; looks like we have engaged and destroyed one sniper vicinity TRP 2 and three or four dismounts vicinity TRP 3."

"Roger. My dismounted section is moving toward TRP 4. I'll move to TRP 2 and see if I can clear the area. Have another patrol clear the other contact."

"Roger that."

We bounded up to the farmhouse, moving in fire teams.

"OP 3, do you have eyes on us?" I whispered into the radio.

The countersniper squad designated marksman responded, "Affirmative. I've got you. Be advised I engaged one individual, second-story window."

We moved up to the house, but the farmer and his family were nowhere to be found. We stacked up on the wall, and I passed forward a signal to breach by squeezing the thigh of the man in front of me. Then the number-four man rushed forward and kicked open the flimsy metal door. We rushed in, clearing the lower room in a matter of seconds. My heart pounded as I stepped smoothly through to positions of dominance, sweeping my rifle across the room. I remembered my old ROTC instructor telling me, "Slow is smooth and smooth is fast." He was a special-forces operator before he came to teach cadets, and he was damn right. The section moved like water—not frantically or choppily, but swiftly between rooms, methodically clearing their sectors for enemy. Then the section split up and slipped up the stairs, leaving two men to hold the lower level. Shouts of "Clear!" echoed through the second floor, followed by the section sergeant.

"Sir, we've got one dead guy up here."

The insurgent was lying across a small table, his rifle, an SVD with a scope, still aimed at the outpost, and his head against the stock. He might as well have been alive and preparing to shoot—except for a small, dark hole near his right eye and a rather large exit wound.

As we marked the building with an orange panel and chem light, I radioed the OP to report the dead sniper. "OP 3, this is Red 1. Good shot—you got a sniper up here."

"Roger that," he responded.

My use of a countersniper position had worked. The enemy shooter could have taken out one of my guys, but instead OP 3 had observed the glint from his scope and sent one round of match-grade 5.56 from the M-16A4 squad designated marksman weapon into his skull. We bagged the dead AIF in a poncho and brought his weapon back to the outpost. I also took some photos of the scene, in case the squadron could use some of this info.

When I reached the outpost, the platoon sergeant briefed me on the other engagement. It seemed that the Bradley on the TCP had spotted suspicious movement and then passed the target to the Bradley at the main gate. The AIF tried to get in a good position to fire off RPGs and an RPK machine gun; they popped off a couple rounds with their AKs, but they were cut down by the 25-mm.

I was excited that all our hard work on countersniper and defensive fortifications had paid off, but frustrated that I was seeing attacks despite trying to talk to the locals. I was amped from the action, and I was getting angry. My men could have gotten hurt; I could have gotten hurt. The insurgents who attacked us were coming from al-Doreaa, so the townspeople had to know who and where they were. The locals must be supporting them. Who the hell did they think they were? It seemed to me that smiling and shaking hands wasn't getting us anywhere. Maybe we just need to root them out house by house.

I called the platoon sergeant over. "We're going to cordon and search every house on the south side of that village. I'm going to show these people what happens when the outpost gets attacked! Figure out a minimal manning plan for the outpost and put together an element for tonight at 0200."

I yelled for my interpreter so that he could prepare for the mission. It was important that all the locals understand my message. Nasir, however, was nowhere to be seen. After a brief scan around the main building I began to worry. The platoon sergeant made a lap around the outpost and reported back. "Sir, one of the guys spotted him running into town after we got attacked." Apparently, Nasir had been pacing around the outpost earlier that day as if taking measurements, and another Soldier claimed that he saw him pass a note to some young Iraqi guy on the street during the patrol. Luckily, we had avoided setting patterns and changed our switch-out times while Nasir was outside the wire with me. But it seemed likely that our interpreter had been gathering intelligence and assisting the enemy. I ordered the platoon sergeant to search the other interpreter and restrict his movement on the COP. I sat down in the main building, resting up for the evening.

At 0200, we set out. The outpost was minimally manned with the mortarmen and a section of Bradleys. I had two HMMWVs with crew served weapons traveling with a dismounted element consisting of three fire teams. My plan was simple: we would start in the east and proceed westward, clearing all the houses and catching the bastards who had been supporting yesterday's attacks. I instructed the team leaders to make sure that people felt the pinch of what happens when they harbor insurgents. I wanted those houses turned upside down.

We started on the first house, which had a tall gate and wall around its front yard. We used the HMMWV to smash the gate and then rushed into the yard to the home. My men breached the front door with a shotgun and then blitzed into the house. I waited outside for command and control and watched as one of my NCOs dragged a skinny, middle-aged man in his nightshirt outside with his hands zip-tied behind his back. After he was thrown to the ground, he looked up at me in despair; I noticed that his nose was bleeding. When I heard "Clear!" come back out the front door, I stepped inside. In the first room three young girls huddled in the corner with their mother, all of them screaming. My Soldiers were searching the house: overturning the mattresses, dumping drawers out of dressers, and shattering furniture. I went outside to find that the skinny man was being questioned by one of my NCOs and our second interpreter.

"We know that you know who is doing these things! Tell us now!" he yelled.

The man was crying and stammering; he didn't seem to know anything of value. For a brief second I wondered how I would feel if I had been pulled out of my house in the middle of the night and humiliated in front of my family.

We went through ten houses in much the same way. In our wake we left broken doors and gates, torn mattresses, broken furniture, and weeping locals. When we used a demolition breach on the last house, I felt the concussion of the charge. The metal door blasted inward and swung violently on its hinges. We entered the house and found an old man lying on the floor by the shattered door. He was covered with wounds from metal shards blasted into the room. After calling the medic forward so we could treat the Iraqi, I stepped back outside, sickened by what I had just seen.

As the sun came up, I called for the platoon sergeant and we went over the numbers. We had searched 11 houses. We'd found 8 poorly maintained AK-47s, one per house, all officially authorized for self-defense. We had zip-cuffed and questioned 26 military-aged men ranging from 16 to 45 years old, and we had found one house that had an old schoolbook with a picture of Saddam in it.

///////////

The next day was uneventful; no sign of enemy activity. After that, everything seemed to change. We began to take contact every day. Patrols began taking direct fire, the outpost received mortar fire once or twice a night, and we engaged two VBIEDs at the checkpoints. We identified IEDs on the route and killed some AIF emplacing them, but some IEDs managed to go off on our resupply convoys. We weathered the attacks and performed well, but it started to feel like we were walking in place; I wondered if we were making the area secure. Some of the Soldiers began complaining that they were just going on patrol to get blown up or draw fire.

A few weeks later the commander arrived on a visit and had a fairly one-sided discussion with me.

"Do you know that you have increased attacks down here by 75%, Lieutenant?"

I gulped and felt a burning in my gut. "No."

"Well, it's true. Whatever you're doing is creating more insurgents; and your men can't sustain this level of contact forever. I'm replacing you with White Platoon. The squadron commander is very concerned about your methods down here. The provincial governor has specifically asked him about our activities in al-Doreaa. Pack up and prepare to RIP with White by tomorrow morning."

I was crushed. How could I have failed when I hadn't taken a single casualty and had defeated countless enemy attacks? Tactically we had performed well, but we still missed the mark. Pondering as I packed my rucksack, I derived four more lessons.

10. To gain the trust and confidence of the local population, you must understand their culture. Plan and rehearse negotiations to ensure success with local leaders.

11. Win early victories.[1] Have a plan to show good faith and authority with the population within your area of responsibility.

12. Maintain operational security. Do not needlessly divulge operational information to people without proper clearances, and do not make it easy for the enemy to gather intelligence on your operations.

13. Avoid knee-jerk reactions; base your actions on good intelligence.[2] Striking out blindly at the population is playing into the insurgent's plan and can only further alienate the people. The counterinsurgent should seek to make no new enemies.

I shoved my toiletry kit into the top of my rucksack and found myself pushing the CO's door open and into another dream.

---

1. David Kilcullen, "Twenty Eight Articles: Fundamentals of Company-Level Counterinsurgency," *Military Review (May–June 2006): 6.*

2. Ibid., 5.

# THE FIFTH DREAM

Do not try to do too much with your own hands. Better the Arabs do it tolerably than you do it perfectly. It is their war, and you are to help them, not to win it for them. Actually, also, under the very odd conditions of Arabia, your practical work will not be as good as, perhaps, you think it is.

—T. E. Lawrence, *The Arab Bulletin*, August 20, 1917

Once again I found myself receiving basically the same mission briefing, and I left my commander's office after requesting interpreters, barrier material, and EOF kits. This time I also requested fifty humanitarian-aid bags to hand out to the local population as a sign of goodwill; I figured that would be a quick way to show our intentions were good. In preparation for my meetings with the population in zone, I took the time to review some basic cultural information from my Iraq Country Handbook. Once again I inspected the platoon, reviewed the ROE, and made sure that language cards were distributed.

We moved down to the outpost and established our defense and patrols. I inspected all the positions and then reviewed the next day's meetings with our interpreter, Nasir. Concerned about maintaining good operational security, I first asked him if he had a cell phone. He said he did. I explained that he would only be able to use the phone once a day, and would have to sign it out from my CP every time he used it. He would also have to stay with us at all times, and would not be allowed to leave the outpost unescorted. Nasir said he understood the need for these measures. With that we rehearsed Iraqi customs and courtesies and reviewed the procedure we planned to follow when we met local leaders. (I was surprised to learn, for example, that using the left hand for eating and gesturing was considered unclean, because that hand is reserved for hygiene.) I selected one of my Soldiers, SPC Wilson, a street-smart guy from Philadelphia, to act as my note taker and second set of eyes during these meetings. I figured he could keep better notes since he wouldn't have to talk, and he would be able to catch things I may miss.

The next morning Wilson, Nasir, and I entered al-Doreaa with a section of men and encountered the mayor and the imam outside the mayor's house. I remembered what we had rehearsed.

"Salaam 'aleikum," I said, extending my hand. "Ismi mulazim Connors. Aliekum assalaam." Both men shook my hand. After introducing themselves, they invited us into the mayor's house.

Once inside, I removed my helmet and ballistic glasses and told my RTO to monitor the radio. The mayor motioned for me to be seated, so Nasir, Wilson, and I sat down in the large meeting room. I paid close attention to my feet and my posture. Despite some discomfort, I managed to keep the soles of my feet facing away from our hosts. Nasir had recommended that I start any meeting with small talk.

"It is an honor to meet you gentlemen. You have a

lovely village." After allowing Nasir time to translate, I continued, "I have a river like this back home. I used to fish every summer when I was a kid."

The mayor smiled broadly and responded, "It is glorious that you are here. Thank you for all that you do. Yes, the village is very nice; I have lived here my whole life. Have you ever had Iraqi fish?"

"No, I have never had the pleasure."

"One day you will come here, and I will have this fish for you."

At this point a boy came from the back room with a tray of chai. I plucked a hot glass from the tray and placed it in front of me on the floor. I stirred the mound of sugar at the bottom of the glass into the liquid. For a moment I wondered if they used river water to make the tea, but remembering my preparation with Nasir, I said "shukran" and took a sip. It really wasn't that bad although, given the hundred-degree weather, I would have preferred an iced cappuccino.

I sipped the chai and the imam asked me, "Do you have children, Lieutenant?"

I refrained from any sort of barracks humor about illegitimate offspring. "I do not. I am not yet married, but I hope to one day have a family. My sister has two children, and I care for them often." With that I pulled out a snapshot of my niece and nephew. The mayor and the imam seemed excited to see the picture.

"I have three children," the mayor said. "One boy and two girls."

"That is very good." I paused to take a sip of chai. "How is the village? Is it safe here for your family?"

"The village is in very bad condition. We have no running water and electricity goes on and off. We have no clinic here and I cannot even care for my own family. My youngest daughter has been sick for a week, but it is dangerous to go to Baghdad for the hospital."

The imam simply nodded his head in agreement.

"Listen, you Americans have come here with many promises, and I have seen nothing."

I was about to tell him how I was going to be different when the food arrived. The chai boy and a teenaged boy brought in a large tin platter and placed it in the center of the floor. A layer of rice covered the plate, and cuts of lamb still on the bone lay on top of it; the meat seemed greenish, or a pale gray in places, from having been boiled instead of grilled. In the center of the plate was a split lamb's head with both eyes boiled to a white haze. I shuddered at the sight of that head staring at me, but to appease my hosts I reached out with my right hand and ate a bit of the vile creature. The boiled meat was chewy and somewhat slimy, but it wasn't too bad. Once we had eaten, I excused myself.

"Thank you, gentlemen; I'm afraid that I have to get back to the outpost."

Everyone rose, and I shook hands as I made my way to the door. The mayor dove in for a pair of kisses, but I was ready for it and met him with a couple of my own. *When in Rome*, I thought. As I felt his unshaven cheek brush against mine and smelled the cheap cologne, I thought of a way to "win an early victory."

"Is your daughter here, sir? I asked.

"She is in the house . . . why do you ask?"

"I have a medic with me. Can we look at your daughter and see if we can help her?"

The mayor's face lit up. He ran into the house, returning after a short time with a small girl wearing a blue nightshirt and a light-blue headscarf.

Before our medic approached her, I warned the mayor. "He will need to touch her; is this okay?"

"Of course; he is a doctor, yes?"

"He is a medic."

Doc asked what the problem was, using Nasir to translate. The girl showed him two large boils about half the size of a golf ball on her leg. Doc took her temperature and checked her vitals. He whispered to me that he would need to drain the boils and administer antibiotics for her fever. I told Nasir to explain this to the mayor, and the mayor agreed. He held down his daughter on the floor of the main room as Doc wiped down the boils with alcohol, pulled out a scalpel, and made a small incision in the first boil. Squeezing it firmly, he drained yellow and white fluid from the wound. At this, the brave little girl started crying openly. Doc moved on to the second boil. Finally, he covered the wounds with antiseptic cream and bandaged them.

While Doc handed a small stack of bandages and tape to the mayor, I confirmed that we would be back to check on his daughter in a couple of days.

"I enjoyed our meeting today."

"Thank you, thank you so much!"

That evening, when I sat down with Nasir, Wilson, and the patrol leaders to review the day, I told them I thought things had gone well.

"Sir, I think you made a good impression, Wilson said. "I can't believe you ate that goat head!"

"If Mayor Hussein is really in charge, he cannot be

trusted. He must know who is conducting attacks near this village," Nasir pointed out. "I think he knows."

"That's right. And that's exactly why I need him on my side. If he knows the insurgents, then maybe he can control them. We'll go back and check on his daughter tomorrow."

Red 2 chimed in: "The HA bags worked great, sir; I was pretty popular walking through the village. I used the other interpreter to talk to a couple of old guys near the center of town. They told me that the town used to be very peaceful before outsiders arrived to conduct attacks."

"I heard the same kind of thing, sir," Red 5 said. "I had a guy tell me that the south side of town is dangerous at night."

That all sounded pretty vague, but it was a start. I was contemplating our next move when we were interrupted by the whiz and crash of 60-mm rounds impacting around the outpost. My platoon, which had rehearsed its response, took cover and moved to the closest position to prepare for a complex attack. The RTO on duty contacted Troop and put in an immediate request for troops in contact AH-64 support.

The platoon members either dove into hardened positions or into vehicles, according to plan, but PVT Witken wasn't so lucky. He was running to help man the southwest machine gun when a round landed just to his right, and he disappeared into a flash of light and a cloud of flying dirt. Another Soldier and I found him lying on the ground. We each grabbed a shoulder and began dragging him back to the cover of the main building, quickly realizing with horror that his legs were still where we had found him; his two bloody, torn stumps were dragging in the dirt. The jagged shrapnel had torn off Witken's legs above the knees. When we reached the inside of the building behind cover, I began applying a tourniquet to his left leg and then to his right.

The man with me slumped to the ground with his head in his hands, rocking back and forth in gentle sobs. I looked up and turned toward Witken's face. His eyes were open but unseeing. A black feeling hovered over the dimly lit room. This seemed the ultimate indignity: a disgusting end to the beautiful thing called life.

As the explosions subsided, the dust began to settle. I was covered in dust and blood, my hands striped with dirt and dark-red stains from Witken's wounds. My chest heaved as I tried to exhale the smells of dirt, carnage, and cordite. I was sorry for Witken, but more than that I was becoming angry.

I felt a burning, frantic, almost animal anger. I wanted to kill them all. I thought I could do it. *That damn village knows exactly who was conducting attacks in this zone. They know who killed Witken! They're probably celebrating, like children who had gotten one over on their parents. Well, I'll show them who's in charge!* Then I remembered something: "Striking out blindly at the population is playing into the insurgent's plan." *If I tear through that town, I will have done what they want, and I will create more enemies.* As I processed this paradox, the rest of the platoon was beginning to come by the body.

"We should kill 'em all. Just unload the 25-mm into the town."

"Fuck these people. Goddamn animals."

I knew this was going to be tough. I went to my

ruck and pulled out a towel to wash off my face. I told the platoon sergeant to bring all the section sergeants in. This is what I told them: "Alright, guys, so you all know we lost Witken tonight. No one did anything wrong; he was just unlucky, and that's what happens. Now the men are going to want blood. I want blood. But we can't give in to it; we cannot blindly go after every Iraqi in zone. We will get the men who did this, but it will take patience and determination. If we hurt the wrong people, we will have created more enemies. Tell everyone that we will follow the ROE, and we will treat the locals with respect. And tell them that I promise we will find these men and make them pay." The sergeants didn't like what I said, but they respected it and they understood.

That night a Blackhawk was dispatched with an Apache in support. A group of us carried Witken's remains in a black body bag from the outpost to the LZ. As the body was loaded into the helicopter and before it disappeared from view, members of the platoon saluted from their positions. I struggled to keep steady in the rotor wash as the bird lifted off into the night sky.

The next day I went to see Mr. Hussein, and Doc checked on his little girl again. I sat down in the mayor's house and he sat across from me.

"I cannot thank you enough for taking care of my daughter," he said through Nasir.

"I would like to help the town like I have helped your daughter, but right now it is very dangerous here."

Mr. Hussein moved closer to me. "I heard about the attack last night. I am very sorry. Was someone hurt?"

"I lost a Soldier last night."

Now he whispered: "I only want peace for this area. I, like you, just want to fish and spend time with my family. I know you have a good heart. You have cared for my family. I promise you that no one from this village did this thing last night."

"Then who did it?" I was trying to control my anger.

"Some young men in this village do not have jobs and can be persuaded to do things by outsiders. It is possible that some outsiders have come here to cause trouble."

"Where can I find these men?"

He drew in even closer. "There is a house with a blue gate near the end of the village." He pointed west.

"Can you show me which house exactly?"

He shook his head wildly. "No, no, no. I have said enough. This is very dangerous."

We finished another round of chai and I returned to the outpost, taking the scenic route. We found three houses with blue gates.

That night I sat down with the patrol leaders again. Red 2 started off.

"We didn't find much, but I talked to the old guys again, and they said bad guys move around after midnight near the road. Sorry that doesn't help much."

Red 5 jumped in: "Well, I'm not sure if this helps, but a guy came up to us while we were on patrol today and said that men in one of the houses were storing weapons. He pointed out the third house from the end, on the west side by the road."

"Did it have a blue gate?"

"Yeah, yeah—I think it did, now that I think about it. But we looked around, peeked over the fence, and didn't see anything out of the ordinary."

"The mayor mentioned possible outsiders in a house on the west side with a blue gate. Let's establish an OP tonight overwatching that side of town. I want to know if we get any movement around this house. I want Alpha and Bravo sections ready to hit the house if we get confirmation tonight."

The RTO woke me around midnight. "Sir, the OP is reporting something on the southwest side of town."

I jumped up to the radio. "This is Red 1. Over."

The reply came in a whisper. "Roger, this is Red 7; I've got one sedan with five males entering building 3. They appear to be transferring items out of the trunk of the vehicle. Can't confirm if it's weapons or not."

It was go time: that made three sources, and I had the house now.

"Get everyone up. We're going to hit the house."

We stalked in from the south, using night-vision goggles. I was with the assault team, and the platoon sergeant was with the inner cordon. The cordon scrolled across the road and moved into position to the west. We sprinted from shadow to shadow along the south side of the buildings toward the target. I spotted the blue gate under the hazy yellow glow of an outdoor light. Red 7 called up as I lit up the door with an IR light.

"Roger, that's it!"

I gave Red 2 the thumbs up, and he blitzed to the door with his four-man stack. The RTO called back to the Bradleys. They began roaring down from the outpost to the target house. The breach man cut the lock on the gate, and Red 2's team smoothly moved inside. From the edge of the gate I heard the blast of the shotgun on the front-door hinges. I entered the courtyard as Red 2 pushed through the building.

That's when the shooting started: a burst of AK fire followed by a flurry of M-4 fire. I saw one man with an AK-47 climb out of one of the windows and race to the back of the courtyard, toward a gate leading to the dirt street behind the house. I took a shot at him but missed, only to see him jerk unnaturally from his head to his feet as flesh flew off his slender body. The platoon sergeant had opened up on him with the M-240.

I radioed Red 2 but got no response. The Bradleys were now right in position, sealing off the site. I moved into the house at the low ready.

"TWO MEN COMING IN!" I yelled. "RED 2, WHAT'S GOING ON?!"

"We've got it, sir. Just a little trouble with the radio."

The handheld MBTR had been smashed by an AK round. Inside, three Iraqi men were sprawled on the floor with numerous puncture wounds from 5.56 rounds. One man seemed to be uninjured and was zip-tied in the corner of the room.

"Take a look at this, sir." A Soldier opened the door to an adjacent room. Inside was a 60-mm mortar tube, rounds, an RPG launcher, and a PKC machine gun. "Looks like we got 'em, sir."

After that raid, we were not attacked again. The days went by, and I worked with the commander to get a medical team down to the village. The mayor and I had dinner every week, planning future improvements. I arranged for clean drinking water to be delivered using our commander's emergency relief funds. I felt we had succeeded in our mission. The village and the area were secure, and the people were conducting their lives in safety and security. It was at about this time that I got the call on the radio.

"Red 1, this is 6. You've done great work down there, and I need your combat power up north. Since your area has cooled down, we need the help up here. Have the platoon up here on the FOB by tomorrow."

I was a caught a little off guard, but I figured he was right. We weren't getting any contact. It seemed like it was time to move on.

The next day, I met with the mayor to let him know we were leaving. When he heard the news, he went pale, gazing at me almost as if he were looking through me. *He'll be fine*, I thought; the village had been quiet for a long time, and it seemed the insurgency had come to an end in al-Doreaa. We rolled back to our original FOB to start packing up for our next mission.

Several days later, I was watching TV in the chow hall when I saw the footage on the news. I recognized the buildings and the bridge at al-Doreaa as the newscaster quickly summarized the scene.

"A small village on the outskirts of Baghdad was seized early this morning, according to film found on a radical Islamic Web site. Video on the site shows masked men moving freely through the town and the public execution of several men."

The images flashed in front of me. Men in masks brandishing AK-47s were walking the streets and firing in the air in triumph. Next I saw the mayor and many of the locals we had cultivated as informants; their hands and feet had been tied behind their backs, and they lay on the street in front of Mr. Hussein's house, with two masked men standing behind them. Everyone who helped us defeat the insurgents and improve security was lined up in a helpless, pathetic heap before the boasting criminals. One man put a pistol against the mayor's head . . . then the screen faded back to the newscaster.

I sat, incredulous, in front of my breakfast of Lucky Charms and wondered how this could have happened. I had had complete control of that area. Everything had gone so well. I remained in the air-conditioned dining facility on the FOB for some time, gradually realizing that we had missed a key element to lasting victory.

14. Counterinsurgency requires a concerted effort between the military, non-governmental organizations, the host nation government, and other elements of national power. Military efforts on their own cannot create enduring success.

15. Protecting established informants prevents their persecution and ensures they can continue to help their neighborhoods even after coalition forces leave.

16. Transition is primary! To achieve lasting success, the security and government functions of your area of operations must be transferred to local security forces and local government officials.

The bits of cereal swirled about in the milk as I found myself swirling into yet another dream.

# THE SIXTH DREAM

You can always count on Americans to do the right thing—
after they've tried everything else.

—Winston Churchill

I entered the commander's office for a sixth time, armed
with sixteen lessons etched into my mind. I received
the mission.

"Do you have any questions?" my commander
asked.

"Sir, I have a few issues . . . I am concerned about
the defense of the site. I would like additional barrier
material, sniper screens, sandbags, wire, trip flares, and
a couple of EOF kits to secure it."

"No problem. Talk to the XO; he'll get you the materials before you roll."

"Also, sir, if I am to secure this whole area, including
the town, I will need interpreters to get intel from the
locals. And if I could get some additional medical supplies and humanitarian aid bags, that might start things
out on the right foot down there."

"I'll call Squadron and coordinate for two interpreters
for your element. Pick up the HA bags from the FSO."

"Sorry to seem needy, sir, but what is the situation
with ISF in the area?"

"The Iraqi 2nd Brigade has a company paired with
our squadron's battle space. They are supposed to take

over the zone eventually, but right now they can barely tie their shoes."

"What are the odds of getting some ISF help in my AO?"

The CO paused. "I'll see what I can do. I have a meeting with General Jassim later this week to coordinate patrols. But don't get your hopes up."

"Thanks, sir; I'll get the platoon moving."

I spent some extra time preparing before I pulled the platoon in for the operations order. Going over the rules of engagement and the escalation of force procedures, I tasked the sections to rehearse the steps before we SP'ed. I also provided details on specific Iraqi tribes and cultural norms in the AO. I ended the briefing with a reminder:

"Gentlemen, we must gain the trust and confidence of the local population to achieve a secure environment. Without their active or passive support, the bad guys can't survive. Separating the insurgents from the population will be a frustrating and difficult task, but it can be done. Our goal is to make no enemies. We want to end each day with fewer insurgents than we started with."[3]

We headed out of the FOB, establishing the outpost for the sixth time. The barriers were emplaced; the cones, wire, and signs signaled to those on the roads that they were approaching a U.S. checkpoint. Sandbags were filled and the position was fortified. I walked the line, refining the defense, clarifying sectors of fire, and checking sector sketches. Patrols with reconnaissance tasks began

3. David Petraeus, "Learning Counterinsurgency: Observations from Soldiering in Iraq," *Military Review (January–February 2006)*: 6.

that evening shortly after the outpost was set in. I posted the platoon fire plan in the building next to the radios. Nasir and I spent the evening rehearsing meetings we would have with the local town leadership.

The RTO shook me awake at about 0500.

"Sir, patrol reports eight men in masks with weapons moving toward the outpost along the river to the east."

I stumbled to the hand mike. "This is Red 1. Over."

A whispering voice replied. "This is Red 7. I've got dismounts moving toward your position along the river in sector B1. Break. I am currently set in OP just east of TRP 3. Over."

"Roger. Can you make it back into the perimeter? Over."

"Negative, negative. Will be compromised if we move."

"Go to ground vicinity TRP 3. Mark your position with IR strobe. Over."

"Wilco."

I turned to the RTO. "Get on the horn to Troop. We're going to need attack aviation. Tell them troops in contact."

The RTO moved to the other hand mike while I addressed the platoon: "All elements go to 100% security. AIF moving in B1."

The positions responded in sequence. I moved from cot to cot waking up the men. As I donned my body armor and Kevlar, I could feel the knot in my stomach clenching down with the anticipation of combat. I loaded and charged a thirty-round magazine of 5.56. I quickly walked out of the dimly lit main building into the early morning darkness. A greenish glow was beginning to appear on the eastern horizon, but it was still hard to see. I approached the massive metal form of a Bradley stationed at position 6. Its diesel engine made a low repeating growl as it idled. I was happy to see the turret moving slowly back and forth, scanning intently for approaching enemy. I rapped at the back hatch until it swung open, held by one of the crew members.

"Morning; are you tracking Red 7's position?"

The young Soldier turned and yelled up into the turret. "Sergeant! Hey, Sir wants to know if we know where Red 7 is."

The sergeant in the turret hollered back over the noise of the machine. "Roger. We're tracking he's near TRP 3."

"You are weapons hold, you must request permission to fire into B2." I didn't want any friendly fire incidents.

The message was relayed up to the turret and I was sure they understood.

I continued to position 2. Manned by two of the mortarmen, it was now reinforced by three more Soldiers who were straining to see their adversaries in the weak light. I heard gunfire to the north.

The explosion that followed was deafening. I could just make out a plume of smoke and dust rising from the north side of the outpost. I clutched the radio hand mike.

"Position 4, SITREP! Position 4, SITREP!"

"Roger . . . one VBIED engaged and destroyed, vicinity position 4."

"Do we have any friendly BDA, over?"

"Negative, negative friendly BDA. We got it at the trigger line. No friendly casualties."

"Roger, continue to maintain security. We will exploit the site after we deal with these dismounts."

I took up a firing position next to the men, resting my weapon on the dew-covered sandbags. A hazy mist was hanging just above the river and melting into a light haze over the high reeds on the bank. The team members at position 2 were riveted to their sectors of fire. I held the buttstock of my rifle against my cheek and scanned with my magnified ACOG sight. I saw a figure rise from the reeds and grass. He was dressed in black, with a black ski mask covering his face. He had an RPG launcher over his right shoulder, and he brought the system to bear on the six of us. As the illuminated triangle reticule of my ACOG covered his chest through the sight, my finger moved from the ready to the trigger. Then I saw him lurch backward, struck by a round. Two more shots rang out. The marksman on the roof had engaged first. I adjusted my aim, working to identify other insurgents.

I fired a couple rounds as the rest of the enemy opened up. The M-240B raked them in well-aimed bursts. A brave few tried to return our fire—a couple of shots whizzed past our heads—but they were quickly cut down. Under heavy fire, four insurgents tried to break contact; three of them were killed as soon as they stood up to move. The fourth was able to dive into the reeds by the riverbank and disappear to the east. I waved my hand across my face and yelled, "CEASE FIRE! CEASE FIRE!"

I called over the platoon net. "All Red elements, we are now weapons hold on the east side; I say again, weapons hold. Break. Red 7, Red 1, over."

"This is Red 7."

"Red 7, we have one AIF moving from position 2 east through B1. Move to kill or capture. Over."

"This is Red 7; moving."

I had started to check for casualties when the radio crackled again.

"Red 1, this is Blumax 26, over."

"This is Red 1."

"And roger, sir. Blumax 26 with a flight of two AH-64s entering your zone in approximately 5 minutes, with 16 Hellfire, 38 rockets, 1 hour 30 minutes' station time, requesting friendly situation and task purpose."

It was the aircraft coming on station.

"Blumax, this is Red 1; I have one platoon at the outpost vicinity grid MR123456 and one team of nine personnel to our east. We have had VBIED and small-arms contact for the last 30 minutes."

I was going to vector them in on our remaining contact in the east when I heard the mortars. The thud of the launch was clearly on the other side of the river.

"INCOMING!" I yelled in unison with what seemed like the whole platoon.

The first round landed in the middle of the outpost. I grabbed the radio. "Blumax, Red 1; I have mortar contact south side of the river, mortar contact south side of the river!"

"Tally that. Five personnel with mortars on south side. Engaging now with rockets."

An Apache roared down the line of the river at tree level and banked hard left over our position. A second Apache came in at a higher angle: *wushhhha wushhha wusssssha*. Hazy smoke stretched in a thin line from the aircraft to the ground as it discharged missiles. The thuds of the impacts caused the platoon to cheer wildly as we stood up from our positions to watch the action.

"Three enemy destroyed, going in for second run."

The first Apache had come back around from the north, and the steady *thrap thrap thrap* of the chain gun filled the air, followed by explosions from the 30-mm high-explosive rounds on the mortar site.

"Red 1, this is Blumax 26. I have BDA 5 enemy personnel and 1 mortar system destroyed; what else do you have for us?"

"Great work. Can you check our perimeter for any additional AIF? Be advised I have one nine-man team looking for one AIF to the east along the river."

"Acknowledged, checking your perimeter now."

I ran to the building and met up with the platoon sergeant. We had zero casualties at that point, and he already had a team preparing to recon the mortar site.

"Red 7, this is Red 1. SITREP, over."

"Red 1, Red 7; we have one detainee. Stand by."

I was happy about that, and I headed toward the Bradleys to check out the VBIED. Outside the compound sat a burning hulk next to the orange cone marking the EOF trigger line for the Bradleys. I was about to congratulate the crews when the radio squelched again.

"Red 1, this is Red 7. We have one detainee with one AK-47. We are moving back to the outpost now."

The Apaches came back up: "Red 1, this is Blumax 26. We have negative contact along your perimeter. We have eyes on your element with the detainee. Over."

"Roger that; I'm moving a team across the bridge to

exploit the mortar site. Protect that element to enable site exploitation. Over."

"This is Blumax 26; Wilco."

I spotted Red 7 and his team crossing the road, entering the outpost from the east. I went back inside to take a look at the detainee. He was covered in mud, and the blood of his friends still covered his shirt and face. He was young, maybe twenty years old, with a baby face; sitting there with his hands zip-cuffed behind his back, he looked more like a curfew violator than a terrorist. We cleaned off his face and worked on the detainee procedures (mug shot, retinal scan, and fingerprints). Then Nasir and I started to ask him questions.

"What is your name?"

"Jamail al-Jabori," he answered softly.

"How many were with you?"

"Six."

"Where are you from?"

"Al-Doreaa."

"Why did you attack us?"

He didn't answer.

"Do you have a job?"

"No."

"Who told you to attack? Who is in charge of you?"

"Kassim . . . Kassim."

"Who is Kassim?"

No answer.

"Who is Kassim?"

Nasir jumped in: "Sir, I don't think this guy he will tell you anything; he knows he is in trouble. This guy is just a kid."

Agreeing with Nasir, I had the mortarmen take him

out to the site of the attack. They took his photo with his AK-47 in front of his fellow insurgents' corpses, with the RPG and other weapons still lying on the ground. I figured this "money shot" would help with prosecution.

We completed site exploitation, collecting evidence and photos. The squadron QRF composed of a platoon of four gun trucks and EOD arrived to help with the effort. We handed off the detainee and the data to the QRF for processing by the S2 shop. EOD checked out the VBIED and took photos and shrapnel; we used a Bradley to push the VBIED carcass off the road. Once things were under control, I figured this was a good opportunity to get back to my original plan and visit the local population. *Maybe some intel could prevent future attacks*, I thought. I was preparing for the dismounted patrol when four Toyota pickups full of Iraqi soldiers, also called Jundees, pulled up to the outpost.

The Jundees wore desert-tan uniforms with the old chocolate-chip pattern from Desert Storm days. Most of them had body armor of one kind or another. They carried AKs, except for one man with a pistol holstered on his hip, who walked up to me.

"Hello, I am Lieutenant Habir. I have been assigned to this post. Are you Lieutenant Connors?" He spoke heavily accented English.

"Yes, I am. And I'm glad to see you."

We sat down on a couple of MRE boxes in the outpost courtyard, where he informed me of his unit's status. He had arrived with four Toyota trucks, four PKCs, and 20 personnel, all armed with AK-47s. He had a basic load of ammunition; food for his men was to be picked up daily from a town north of our position. I brought

Habir up to speed on the events of the morning, and we designated an area for his forces to set up their gear and park their vehicles. We also decided that, after they had established themselves, we would integrate them into the defense.

"I was about to go into town and meet the local leaders. Would you like to go with me?"

"Sure, sure, this is a good idea."

He grabbed two of his men to join me and my patrol.

As we walked through al-Doreaa, I was surprised to find that the Jundees seemed at ease and spoke freely with the locals. It became clear that their knowledge of Arabic and of the Iraqi people was something we couldn't ever fully replicate. When we passed near the

food stands Habir was approached by a short man with a thick mustache who shook his hand heartily and kissed him on the cheeks. "This is my cousin Ahmed; he lives in this town."

Ahmed reached out his hand to me as Habir introduced me in Arabic. Ahmed invited us to his home, and soon our patrol let him lead the way there. I noticed a new satellite dish in his yard, next to a chicken coop. Once we were settled inside Ahmed's home, Nasir translated for me as Habir and Ahmed spoke to each other.

"How is your father?" Habir asked.

"He is well. And how is your family, they are well?"

"Yes, fine."

"I didn't expect to find you here. I thought you were in Baghdad. Al-Doreaa is not a safe place." Ahmed's son came into the room and handed out cans of cola. I looked at the can and asked Nasir where it came from.

"This, it is from Iran, I think . . . yes, Iran. It's good, no?"

I took a gulp of the sugary beverage and felt that somehow, in a weird way, I was supporting Hezbollah.

Ahmed now addressed us as well: "I love the Americans, but some here in town have fought the occupation. Now foreigners and criminals have made this place unsafe. People are tired of the violence and want peace."

"I understand, Ahmed, and we are here to help. I am truly here to help Habir bring safety to the town." I pulled out my wallet with photos of my sister, niece, and nephew. "This is my family; I understand the importance of keeping the ones you love from harm. I want nothing more than to make this village safe and allow Iraqis to govern Iraqis."

Ahmed nodded and then looked to the door, rising to greet a new guest. The man introduced himself as Mr. Hussein, the mayor of the village. Habir rattled off some small talk before our discussion again turned to the state of the town.

Mr. Hussein told us that al-Doreaa was "in desperate need of medical care. We need immunizations and a clinic; it is too hard to reach a hospital in Baghdad."

I had hoped he would give me this opportunity. "I have some medical supplies. Do you have a town doctor?"

"No, we do not; this is a big problem."

"I will try to help."

"I will believe it when it happens. I have had many years of promises."

When we had finished our sodas and rose to leave, Habir lingered inside, conversing with his cousin. As soon as he joined us, he pulled me aside. "Phil, my cousin told me of big bad guy in town. He is willing to help us—tonight if we are ready."

Once we had returned to the outpost, I had two pressing priorities: find out how to get medical treatment to the town, and consolidate the intel from today's patrols. I could provide medical care either by using my medics and small package of medical supplies or by getting Squadron to cough up a bigger team, one that would include a physician's assistant and a doctor. Neither option seemed ideal: neither would empower the local government and security forces or aid with transition. But I also needed to win an early victory! Deciding, finally, on a compromise, I tasked the RTO to work out some details with Squadron while I briefed the medics.

Next, I took on the intel issues. I pulled in the squad leaders along with Habir to review the day's events.

The platoon sergeant started. "Sir, we received some intel from higher while you were on patrol. It seems that when EOD went through the VBIED from this morning, they found that the vehicle identification number was linked to a group of vehicles purchased in Syria which have been associated with other bombings. They gave us the name Kassim Fareed, who apparently is the leader of the local Al Qaeda faction. Also looks like the guy we got this morning is singing. He says Kassim lives with a few bodyguards near the Sunni mosque in al-Doreaa. Squadron has made him an HVT."

Habir jumped in. "My cousin also mentioned this name; he says this 'Kassim' moved into the village two weeks ago, killing several villagers. He told me he would show us the house tonight."

"Looks like we have a date with Kassim."

"My element must execute this operation," Habir declared. "It is our country, and we will capture this terrorist."

"Okay, sounds good; but we will provide your outer cordon and some additional firepower with the Bradleys."

Habir and I set a 0400 hit time on the house. At 0330, Habir and his men walked into town, met with his cousin, and quickly moved to a little house on the south side of town. I had a dismount team on the south side of the road and a Bradley section moving into position to support when they entered the building. By 0405 they were exiting the house with four men in zip cuffs. Inside was a cache of rifles and IED-making material. I moved onto the site with the exploitation team and collected the evidence. Ahmed identified one of the men as Kassim Fareed; the insurgents were then picked up by the squadron QRF and moved back to the FOB for interrogation. By 0530, the Iraqis had completed the raid, successfully and on their own. Kassim was off the streets. I was proud to have worked with Habir and his men. My respect for the Iraqis and their way of life truly grew the more I came in contact with them. The clash of civilizations may not be as sharp as I once thought.

After a brief recovery, we returned to the village to meet with the mayor. Habir and I had rehearsed ahead of time; he was prepared to take charge of the discussion. We sat on the floor of Mr. Hussein's house as before, but this time I would not be running the meeting.

Habir began the discussion. "I was able to work with the Americans to assist your people today. As you know, we captured a major criminal in your village this morning. We know that you have been in evil's grip, and this is not your fault."

The mayor responded, "This may be a good thing that this man is gone, and truly the people of this village want peace. But more will come, and I fear that we will suffer for working with you and the Americans."

Habir looked at Mr. Hussein intently. "Now is the time we must choose. Will we choose fear, hatred, and war, or will we choose prosperity and justice? The insurgents have only brought you pain and suffering. Together we can create a better life for the people of Doreaa."

"I have heard these words before. Tell me, how will we protect ourselves when your words and soldiers leave my village?"

"I will need three names of men willing to be trained as police to keep the town safe. First we will train them, and then they will attend the police academy. You will be able to protect yourselves and your family, and we will help."

"This is excellent. You will have them today."

"The Americans have medical supplies to treat thirty villagers today, children and elderly only. But this will not truly help the town. I understand you do not have a doctor?"

"This is true; we have no doctor."

"I will need you to select one man from the town to be trained by the American medics. He will act as your town doctor. Also, I have coordinated with the Health Ministry to have your town inspected as a possible clinic location."

"Thank you! This is wonderful."

The mayor called his son and told him to inform the village about the medical aid. Habir and Mr. Hussein continued to talk pleasantly until a crowd gathered outside the house.

The mayor walked outdoors and into the crowd, selecting the thirty children and elderly people to be treated; he was obviously happy to be empowered by the event. The Iraqi soldiers handled crowd control and our medics administered care to the selected patients while the villagers watched, smiling and hopeful.

Over the following weeks, we continued to assist Habir. He and his men developed a great relationship with the population and gained complete control of the area. The IP candidates received basic skills training at the outpost and were later sent to the academy. The mayor was linked in with the Health Ministry and was able to speak with his provincial leaders to arrange for supplies. We integrated USAID and Doctors Without Borders into our plans, bringing much-needed assistance to the area. Al-Doreaa had turned a corner. Iraqis conducted most of the daylight patrolling, while our platoon focused on night patrols and OPs.

It was at this point that my CO came down to visit. "You've done a great job here, Connors. But it's time to pack it up. We are headed to Haditha to support operations there. The IA are being given control of this AO."

After we packed our gear and lined up to leave, I spoke to Habir for the last time.

"Don't worry about us," he said. "This is our fight, and only we can win it. Thank you for your help. We can take it from here."

Smiling, I climbed into my HMMWV. The mission

had been a success—at least as much of a success as you can achieve in counterinsurgency. Bidding goodbye to Doreaa, I realized that war isn't about glory and Silver Stars; it's about bringing Soldiers home alive and making responsible decisions. Getting in firefights and raiding buildings is exciting, but creating a lasting stability is real victory. . . .

The thud of the wheels hitting the runway woke me, and as I shook off the ungodly effects of the sleeping pills and stretched my stiff arms, blinking at the harsh light of the interior of our aircraft, I realized that I was only just now arriving in Kuwait.

# THE
# DEFENCE
# OF
# DUFFER'S
# DRIFT

## A LESSON IN THE FUNDAMENTALS
## OF SMALL UNIT TACTICS

# BACKGROUND INFORMATION (THE BOER WAR)

The Boers (Dutch for "farmer") first settled in what is now Cape Province, Republic of South Africa, in 1652. After Great Britain annexed this territory in 1806, many of the Boers departed on the "Great Trek" and created the Republic of Natal, the Orange Free State, and the Transvaal. Gradual commercial control by the British and discovery of gold and diamonds, among other things, served to create hostility between the Boers and British, resulting in the South African War, or Boer War, from 1899 to 1902.

The Boers initially outnumbered the British and were well equipped, scoring impressive victories in the areas adjacent to their territories. Even though the Boer armies finally surrendered, apparent victory for the British was retarded by extensive and coordinated guerrilla warfare. The war was finally ended by the systematic destruction of the Boer guerrilla units and hostilities were terminated by the Treaty of Vereeniging in May 1902. The Boer territories were annexed by Great Britain and were organized into the Union of South Africa eight years later.

# GLOSSARY

| | |
|---|---|
| ABATIS | A barricade of felled trees with branches facing the enemy. |
| ANTHILL | A large cone-shaped mound of earth. |
| BOER | Descendents of Dutch colonists in South Africa. |
| DONGA | South African gully or ravine. |
| DRIFT | A ford, a shallow place in a stream or river that can be crossed by walking or riding on horseback. |
| DUFFER | An incompetent, awkward or stupid person. |
| KAFFIR | A fierce black tribe of South Africa (19th century). |
| KOPJE | A rocky hill or butte of South Africa, usually 200–800 meters high. |
| KRAAL | A village of South African natives surrounded by a stockade for protection. |
| QUI VIVE | Fr., a sentry's challenge; "Who goes there?" |
| SUBALTERN | A British officer holding a commission below that of captain; a lieutenant. |
| VELD | A grassy plain of South Africa, similar to the Western Tableland of the United States. |
| V.C. | Victoria Cross, highest British medal for valor. |

# PREFACE

"It was our own fault, and our very grave fault, and now
    we must turn it to use,
We have forty million reasons for failure, but not a
    single excuse!"

—Kipling

This tale of a dream is dedicated to the "gilded Pop-
injays" and "hired assassins" of the British nation, especially those who are now knocking at the door, to
wit the very junior. It embodies some recollections
of things actually done and undone in South Africa,
1899–1902. It is hoped that its fantastic guise may really help to emphasise the necessity for the practical application of some very old principles, and assist to an
appreciation of what may happen when they are not
applied, even on small operations. This practical application has often been lost sight of in the stress of the
moment, with dire results, quite unrealised until the
horrible instant of actual experience. Should this tale,
by arousing the imagination, assist to prevent in the
future even one such case of disregard of principles, it
will not have been written in vain. The dreams are not
anticipations, but merely a record of petty experiences
against one kind of enemy in one kind of country only,
with certain deductions based thereupon. But from
these, given the conditions, it is not difficult to deduce
the variations suitable for other countries, or for those

occasions when a different foe with different methods of fighting and different weapons has to be met.

*"Backsight Forethought"*

*June, 1907*

# PROLOGUE

Upon an evening after a long and tiring trek, I arrived at Dreamdorp. The local atmosphere, combined with a heavy meal, is responsible for the following nightmare, consisting of a series of dreams. To make the sequence of the whole intelligible, it is necessary to explain that though the scene of each vision was the same, by some curious mental process I had no recollection of the place whatsoever. In each dream the locality was totally new to me, and I had an entirely fresh detachment. Thus, I had not the great advantage of working over familiar ground. One thing, and one only, was carried on from dream to dream, and that was the vivid recollection of the general lessons previously learnt. These finally produced success.

The whole series of dreams, however, remained in my memory as a connected whole when I awoke.

# FIRST DREAM

"Any fool can get into a hole."

—Old Chinese Proverb

"If left to you, for defence make spades."

—Bridge Maxim

I felt lonely, and not a little sad, as I stood on the bank of the river near Duffer's Drift and watched the red dust haze, raised by the southward departing column in the distance, turn slowly into gold as it hung in the afternoon sunlight. It was just three o'clock, and here I was on the banks of the Silliaasvogel river, left behind by my column with a party of fifty NCOs and men to hold the drift. It was an important ford, because it was the only one across which wheeled traffic could pass for some miles up or down the river.

The river was a sluggish stream, not now in flood, crawling along at the very bottom of its bed between steep banks which were almost vertical, or at any rate too steep for waggons anywhere except at the drift itself. The banks from the river edge to their tops and some distance outwards, were covered with dense thorn and other bushes, which formed a screen impenetrable to the sight. They were also broken by small ravines and holes, where the earth had been eaten away by the river when in flood, and were consequently very rough.

Map 1

| (1) | SILLIAASVOGEL RIVER | (2) | DRIFT |
| (3) | REGRET TABLE MOUNTAIN | (4) | WASCHOUT HILL |
| (5) | INCIDENTAMBA | (6) | KRAAL |

Some 2000 odd meters north of the drift was a flat-topped, rocky mountain, and about a mile to the north-east appeared the usual sugar-loaf kopje, covered with bushes and boulders—steep on the south, but gently falling to the north; this had a farm on the near side of it.

About 1000 meters south of the drift was a convex and smooth hill, somewhat like an inverted basin, sparsely sown with small boulders, and with a Kaffir kraal, consisting of a few grass mud huts on top. Between the river and the hills on the north the ground consisted of open and almost level veld; on the south bank the veld was more undulating, and equally open. The whole place was covered with anthills.

My orders were to hold Duffer's Drift at all costs. I should probably be visited by some column within three or four days' time. I might possibly be attacked before that time, but this was very unlikely, as no enemy were known to be within a hundred miles. The enemy had guns.

It all seemed plain enough, except that the true inwardness of the last piece of information did not strike me at the time. Though in company with fifty "good men and true," it certainly made me feel somewhat lonely and marooned to be left out there comparatively alone on the boundless veld; but the chance of an attack filled me, and I am quite sure, my men, with martial ardour. At last here was the chance I had so often longed for. This was my first "show," my first independent command, and I was determined to carry out my order to the bitter end. I was young and inexperienced, it is true, but I had passed all my examinations with fair success; my men were a good willing lot, with the traditions of a glorious regiment to uphold, and would, I knew, do all I should require of them. We were also well supplied with ammunition and rations and had a number of picks, shovels, and sandbags, etc., which I confess had been rather forced on me.

As I turned towards my gallant little detachment, vi-

**Map 2**

sions of a bloody and desperate fight crossed my mind—
a fight to the last cartridge, and then an appeal to cold
steel, with ultimate victory and—but a discreet cough at
my elbow brought me back to realities, and warned me
that my colour-sergeant was waiting for orders.

After a moment's consideration, I decided to pitch
my small camp on a spot just south of the drift, because
it was slightly rising ground, which I knew should be

chosen for a camp whenever possible. It was, moreover, quite close to the drift, which was also in its favour, for, as every one knows, if you are told off to guard anything, you mount a guard quite close to it, and place a sentry, if possible, standing on top of it. The place I picked out also had the river circling round three sides of it in a regular horseshoe bend, which formed a kind of ditch, or, as the book says, "a natural obstacle." I was indeed lucky to have such an ideal place close at hand; nothing could have been more suitable.

I came to the conclusion that, as the enemy were not within a hundred miles, there would be no need to place the camp in a state of defence till the following day. Besides, the men were tired after their long trek, and it would be quite as much as they could do comfortably to arrange nice and shipshape all the stores and tools, which had been dumped down anyhow in a heap, pitch the camp, and get their teas before dark.

Between you and me, I was really relieved to be able to put off my defensive measures till the morrow, because I was a wee bit puzzled as to what to do. In fact, the more I thought, the more puzzled I grew. The only "measures of defence" I could recall for the moment were, how to tie "a thumb or overhand knot," and how long it takes to cut down an apple tree of six inches diameter. Unluckily neither of these useful facts seemed quite to apply. Now, if they had given me a job like fighting the battle of Waterloo, or Sedan, or Bull Run, I knew all about that, as I had crammed it up and been examined in it too. I also knew how to take up a position for a division, or even an army corps, but the stupid little subaltern's game of the defence of a drift with a small detachment was, curiously enough, most perplexing, I had never really considered such a thing. However, in the light of my habitual dealings with army corps, it would, no doubt, be child's-play after a little thought.

Having issued my immediate orders accordingly, I decided to explore the neighbourhood, but was for a moment puzzled as to which direction I should take; for, having no horse, I could not possibly get all round before dark. After a little thought, it flashed across my mind that obviously I should go to the north. The bulk of the enemy being away to the north, that of course must be the front. I knew naturally that there must be a front, because in all the schemes I had had to prepare, or the exams I had undergone, there was always a front, or—"the place where the enemies come from." How often, also, had I not had trouble in getting out of a dull sentry which his "front" and what his "beat" was. The north, then, being my front, the east and west were my flanks, where there might possibly be enemies, and the south was my rear, where naturally there were none.

I settled these knotty points to my satisfaction, and off I trudged, with my field-glasses, and, of course, my Kodak, directing my steps towards the gleaming white walls of the little Dutch farm, nestling under the kopje to the north-east. It was quite a snug little farm for South Africa, and was surrounded by blue gums and fruit trees. About a quarter of a mile from the farm I was met by the owner, Mr. Andreas Brink, a tame or surrendered Boer farmer, and his two sons, Piet and Gert, "Such a nice man too," with a pleasant face and long beard. He would insist on calling me "Captain," and as any

correction might have confused him, I did not think it
worth while to make any, and after all I wasn't so very
far from my "company." The three of them positively
bristled with dog's-eared and dirty passes from every
Provost Marshal in South Africa, and these they insisted
on showing me. I had not thought of asking for them,
and was much impressed; to have so many they must
be special men. They escorted me to the farm, where
the good wife and several daughters met us, and gave
me a drink of milk, which was most acceptable after my
long and dusty trek. The whole family appeared either
to speak or to understand English, and we had a very
friendly chat, during the course of which I gathered that
there were no Boer commandos anywhere within miles,
that the whole family cordially hoped that there never
would be again, and that Brink was really a most loyal
Briton, and had been much against the war, but had been
forced to go on commando with his two sons. Their
loyalty was evident, because there was an oleograph of
the Queen on the wall, and one of the numerous flappers
was playing our National Anthem on the harmonium
as I entered.

The farmer and the boys took a great interest in all
my personal gear, especially a brand-new pair of the
latest-pattern field-glasses, which they tried with much
delight, and many exclamations of "Allermachtig." They
evidently appreciated them extremely, but could not im-
agine any use for my Kodak in war-time, even after I had
taken a family group. Funny, simple fellows! They asked
and got permission from me to sell milk, eggs and butter
in the camp, and I strolled on my way, congratulating
myself on the good turn I was thus able to do myself

and detachment, none of whom had even smelt such luxuries for weeks.

After an uneventful round, I directed my steps back towards the thin blue threads of smoke, rising vertically in the still air, which alone showed the position of my little post, and as I walked the peacefulness of the whole scene impressed me. The landscape lay bathed in the warm light of the setting sun, whose parting rays tinged most strongly the various heights within view, and the hush of approaching evening was only broken by the distant lowing of oxen, and by the indistinct and cheerful camp noises, which gradually grew louder as I approached. I strolled along in quite a pleasant frame of mind, meditating over the rather curious names which Mr. Brink had given me for the surrounding features of the landscape. The kopje above his farm was called Incidentamba, the flat-topped mountain some two miles to the north was called Regret Table Mountain, and the gently rising hill close to the drift on the south of the river they called Waschout Hill. Everything was going on well, and the men were at their teas when I got back. The nice Dutchman with his apostolic face and the lanky Piet and Gert were already there, surrounded by a swarm of men, to whom they were selling their wares at exorbitant rates. The three of them strolled about the camp, showing great interest in everything, asking most intelligent questions about the British forces and the general position of affairs and seemed really relieved to have a strong British post near. They did not even take offence when some of the rougher men called them "blarsted Dutchmen," and refused to converse with them, or buy their "skoff." About dusk they left, with many promises to return with a fresh supply on the morrow.

After writing out my orders for next day—one of which was for digging some trenches round the camp, an operation which I knew my men, as becomes good British soldiers, disliked very much, and regarded as fatigues—I saw the two guards mounted, one at the drift, and the other some little way down the river, each furnishing one sentry on the river-bank.

When all had turned in, and the camp was quite silent, it was almost comforting to hear the half-hourly cry of the sentries. "Number one—all is well!; Number two—all is well!" By this sound I was able to locate them, and knew they were at their proper posts. On going round sentries about midnight, I was pleased to find that they were both alert, and that, as it was a cold night, each guard had built a bonfire silhouetted in the cheerful blaze of which stood the sentry—a clear-cut monument to all around that here was a British sentry fully on the *qui-vive*. After impressing them with their orders, the extent of their "beat," and the direction of their "front," etc., I turned in. The fires they had built, besides being a comfort to themselves, were also useful to me, because twice during the night when I looked out I could, without leaving my tent, plainly see them at their posts. I finally fell asleep, and dreamt of being decorated with a crossbelt made of V.C.s and D.S.O.s, and of wearing red tabs all down my back.

I was suddenly awoken, about the grey of dawn, by a hoarse cry, "Halt! who goes. . . ." cut short by the unmistakable "plipplop" of a Mauser rifle. Before I was off my valise, the reports of Mausers rang round the camp from every side, these, mingled with the smack of the bullets as they hit the ground and stripped, the "zipzip" of the leaden hail through the tents, and the curses and groans of men who were hit as they lay or stumbled about trying to get out, made a hellish din. There was some wild shooting in return from my men, but it was all over in a moment, and as I managed to wriggle out of my tent the whole place was swarming with bearded men, shooting into the heaving canvas. At that moment I must have been clubbed on the head for I knew no more until I found myself seated on an empty case having my head, which was dripping with blood, tied up by one of my men.

Our losses were 10 men killed, including both sentries, and 21 wounded; the Boers' had one killed and two wounded.

Later on, as, at the order of the not ill-natured but very frowzy Boer commandant, I was gloomily taking off the saucy warm spotted waistcoat knitted for me by my sister, I noticed our friends of the previous evening in very animated and friendly conversation with the burghers, and "Pappa" was, curiously enough, carrying a rifle and bandolier and my new field-glasses. He was laughing and pointing towards something lying on the ground, through which he finally put his foot. This, to my horror, I recognised as my unhappy camera. Here, I suppose, my mind must have slightly wandered, for I found myself repeating some Latin lines, once my favourite imposition, but forgotten since my school-days—"*Timeo Danaos et dona ferentes. . . .*" when suddenly the voice of the field cornet broke into my musing with "Your breeches too, captain."

Trekking all that day on foot, sockless, and in the boots of another, I had much to think of besides my throbbing head. The sight of the long Boer convoy with guns, which had succeeded so easily in crossing the drift I was to have held, was a continual reminder of my failure and of my responsibility for the dreadful losses to my poor detachment. I gradually gathered from the Boers what I had already partly guessed, namely, that they had been fetched and guided all round our camp by friend Brink, had surrounded it in the dark, crawling about in the bush on the river-bank, and had carefully marked down our two poor sentries. These they had at once shot on the alarm being given, and had then rushed the camp from the dense cover on three sides. Towards evening my head got worse, and its rhythmic throbbing seemed gradually to take a meaning, and hammered out the following lessons, the result of much pondering on my failure:

1. Do not put off taking your measures of defence till the morrow, as these are more important than the comfort of your men or the shipshape arrangement of your camp. Choose the position of your camp mainly with reference to your defence.

2. Do not in war-time show stray men of the enemy's breed all over your camp, be they never so kind and full of butter, and do not be hypnotised, by numerous "passes," at once to confide in them.

3. Do not let your sentries advertise their position to the whole world, including the enemy, by

      standing in the full glare of a fire, and making
      much noise every half-hour.

4. Do not, if avoidable, be in tents when bullets
      are ripping through them; at such times a hole
      in the ground is worth many tents.

After these lessons had been dinned into my soul millions and millions of times, so that I could never forget them, a strange thing came to pass—there was a kaleidoscopic change—I had another dream.

# SECOND DREAM

"And what did ye look they should compass? Warcraft
    learnt in a breath,
Knowledge unto occasion at the first
    far view of
Death?"

    —Kipling


I suddenly found myself dumped down at Duffer's
Drift with the same orders as already detailed, and an
equal detachment composed of entirely different men.
As before, and on every subsequent occasion, I had
ample stores, ammunition, and tools. My position was
precisely similar to my former one, with this important exception—running through my brain were four
lessons.

As soon as I received my orders, therefore, I began
to make out my plan of operations without wasting any
time over the landscape, the setting sun, or the departing
column, which, having off-loaded all our stores, soon
vanished. I was determined to carry out all the lessons
I had learnt as well as I knew how.

To prevent any strangers, friendly or otherwise,
from coming into my position and spying out the elab-
orate defences I was going to make, I sent out at once
two examining posts of one NCO and three men each,
one to the top of Waschout Hill, and the other some
1000 meters out on the veld to the north of the drift.

**Map 3**

Their orders were to watch the surrounding country, and give the alarm in the event of the approach of any body of men whatever (Boers were, of course, improbable, but still just possible), and also to stop any individuals, friendly or not, from coming anywhere near camp and to shoot at once any non-compliance with the order to halt. If the newcomers had any provisions to sell, these were to be sent in with a list by one of the guard, who would return with the money, but the strangers were not to be allowed nearer the camp on any account.

Having thus arranged a safeguard against spies, I proceeded to choose a camping ground. I chose the site already described in my former dream, and for the same reasons, which still appealed to me. So long as I was entrenched, it appeared the best place around. We started making our trenches as soon as I had marked off a nice squarish little enclosure which would about contain our small camp. Though, of course, the north was the front, I thought, having a camp, it would be best to have an all-round defence as a sort of obstacle. The majority of the men were told off to dig, which they did not relish, a few being detailed to pitch camp and prepare tea. As the length of trench was rather great for the available number of diggers, and the soil was hard, we were only able by dark, by which time the men were quite done up by their hard day, to make quite a low parapet and shallow trench. Still we were "entrenched," which was the great thing, and the trench was all round our camp, so we were well prepared, even should we be attacked during the night or early next morning, which was quite unlikely.

During this time one or two strangers had approached the guard of the north from a farm under Incidentamba. As they had eggs and butter, etc., to sell, these were brought in as arranged for. The man sent in with the stuff reported that the elder of the Dutchmen was a most pleasant man, and had sent me a present of a pat of butter and some eggs, with his compliments, and would I allow him to come in and speak to me? However, not being such a fool as to allow him in my defences, I went out instead, in case he had any information. His only information was that there were no Boers anywhere near. He was an old man, but though he had a museum of "passes," I was not to be chloroformed by them into confidence. As he seemed friendly, and possibly loyal, I walked part of the way back to his farm with him, in order to look around. At dark the two examining posts came in, and two guards were mounted close by the object I was to watch, namely, the drift, at the same places as in my previous dream. This time, however, there was no half-hourly shouting, nor were there any fires, and the sentries had orders not to challenge but to shoot any person they might see outside camp at once. They were placed standing down the river-bank, just high enough to see over the top, and were thus not unnecessarily exposed. Teas had been eaten, and all fires put out at dusk, and after dark all turned in, but in the trenches instead of in tents. After going round sentries to see everything snug for the night, I lay down myself with a sense of having done my duty, and neglected no possible precaution for our safety.

Just before dawn much the same happened as already described in my first dream, except that the ball was started by a shot without challenge from one of our sentries at something moving among the bush, which resulted in close-range fire opening up to us from all sides. This time we were not rushed, but a perfect hail of bullets whistled in from every direction—from in front of each trench, and over and through our parapet. It was sufficient to put a hand or head up to have a dozen bullets through and all round it, and the strange part was, we saw no one. As the detachment wag plaintively remarked, we could have seen lots of Boers, "if it wasn't for the bushes in between."

After vainly trying until bright daylight to see the enemy in order to do some damage in return, so many men were hit, and the position seemed so utterly hopeless, that I had to hoist the white flag. We had by then 24 men killed and six wounded. As soon as the white flag went up the Boers ceased firing at once, and stood up; every bush and anthill up to 100 meters range seemed to have hid a Boer behind it. This close range explained the marvellous accuracy of their shooting, and the great proportion of our killed (who were nearly all shot through the head) to our wounded.

As we were collecting ourselves preparatory to marching off there were one or two things which struck me; one was that the Dutchman who had presented me with eggs and butter was in earnest confabulation with the Boer commandant, who was calling him "Oom" most affectionately. I also noticed that all male Kaffirs from the neighbouring kraal had been fetched and impressed to assist in getting the Boer guns and waggons across the drift and to load up our captured gear, and generally do odd and dirty jobs. These same Kaffirs did their work with amazing alacrity, and looked as if they enjoyed it; there was no "backchat" when an order was given— usually by friend "Oom."

Again, as I trudged with blistered feet that livelong day, did I think over my failure. It seemed so strange, I had done all I knew, and yet, here we were, ignominiously captured, 24 of us killed, and the Boers over the drift. "Ah, BF, my boy," I thought, "there must be a few more lessons to be learnt besides those you already know." In order to find out what these were, I pondered deeply over the details of the fight.

The Boers must have known of our position, but how had they managed to get close up all round within snapshooting range without being discovered? What a tremendous advantage they had gained in shooting from among the bushes on the bank, where they could not be seen, over us who had to show up over a parapet every time we looked for an enemy, and show up, moreover, just in the very place where every Boer expected us to. There seemed to be some fault in the position. How the bullets seemed sometimes to come through the parapet, and how those that passed over one side hit the men defending the other side in the back. How, on the whole, that "natural obstacle," the river-bed, seemed to be more of a disadvantage than a protection.

Eventually the following lessons framed themselves in my head—some of them quite new, some of them supplementing those four I had already learnt:

5. With modern rifles, to guard a drift or locality does not necessitate sitting on top of it (as if it could be picked up and carried away), unless the locality is suitable to hold for other and defensive reasons. It may even be much better to take up your defensive position some way from the spot, and so away from concealed ground, which enables the enemy to crawl up to very close range, concealed and unperceived, and to fire from cover which hides them even when shooting. It would be better, if possible, to have

the enemy in the open, or to have what is called a clear "field of fire."

A non-bulletproof parapet or shelter which is visible serves merely to attract bullets instead of keeping them out—the proof of thickness can be easily and practically tested.

When fired at by an enemy at close range from nearly all round, a low parapet and shallow trench are not of much use, as what bullets do not hit the defenders on one side hit those on another.

6. It is not enough to keep strange men of the enemy's breed away from your actual defences, letting them go free to warn their friends of your existence and whereabouts—even though they should not be under temptation to impart any knowledge they may have obtained. "Another way," as the cookery book says, more economical in lives, would be as follows: Gather and warmly greet a sufficiency of stranger. Stuff well with chestnuts as to the large force about to join you in a few hours; garnish with corroborative detail, and season according to taste with whiskey or tobacco. This will very likely be sufficient for the nearest commando. Probable cost—some heavy and glib lying, but no lives will be expended.

7. It is not business to allow lazy men (even though they may be brothers and neutrals) to sit and pick their teeth outside their kraals whilst tired soldiers are breaking their hearts trying to do heavy labour in short time. It is more the

duty of a soldier to teach the lazy neutral the
dignity of labour, and by keeping him under
guard to prevent his going away to talk about it.

By the time the above lessons had been well burnt into
my brain, beyond all chance of forgetfulness, a strange
thing happened. I had a fresh dream.

# THIRD DREAM

"So when we take tea with a few guns, o'course you
    will know what to do—hoo! hoo!"

—Kipling

I was at Duffer's Drift on a similar sunny afternoon and
under precisely similar conditions, except that I now
had seven lessons running through my mind.

I at once sent out two patrols, each of one NCO and
three men, one to the north and one to the south. They
were to visit all neighbouring farms and kraals and bring
in all able-bodied Dutch men and boys and male Kaffirs—by persuasion if possible, but by force if necessary.
This would prevent the news of our arrival being carried
round to any adjacent commandos, and would also assist
to solve the labour question. A small guard was mounted
on the top of Waschout Hill as a look-out.

I decided that as the drift could not get up and run
away, it was not necessary to take up my post or position quite close to it, especially as such a position would
be under close rifle fire from the river-bank, to which
the approaches were quite concealed, and which gave
excellent cover. The very worst place for such a position
seemed to be anywhere within the horseshoe bend of
the river, as this would allow an enemy practically to
surround it. My choice therefore fell on a spot to which
the ground gently rose from the river-bank, some 700
to 800 meters south of the drift. Here I arranged to dig

a trench roughly facing the front (north), which thus would have about 800 meters clear ground on its front. We started to make a trench about 50 meters long for my 50 men, according to the usual rule.

Some little time after beginning, the patrols came in, having collected three Dutchmen and two boys, and about thirteen Kaffirs. The former, the leader of whom seemed a man of education and some importance, were at first inclined to protest when they were given tools to dig trenches for themselves, showed bundles of "passes," and talked very big about complaining to the general, and even as to a question in the "House" about our brutality. This momentarily staggered me, as I could not help wondering what might happen to poor BF if the member for Upper Tooting should raise the point; but Westminster was far away, and I hardened my heart. Finally they had the humour to see the force of the argument, that it was, after all, necessary for their own health, should the post be attacked, as they would otherwise be out in the open veld.

The Kaffirs served as a welcome relief to my men as they got tired. They also dug a separate hole for themselves on one side of and behind our trench, in a small ravine.

By evening we had quite a decent trench dug—the parapet was two feet six inches thick at the top, and was quite bulletproof, as I tested it. Our trench was not all in one straight line, but in two portions, broken back at a slight angle, so as to get a more divergent fire (rather cunning of me), though each half was of course as straight as I could get it.

It was astonishing what difficulty I had to get the men

**Map 4**

to dig in a nice straight line. I was particular as to this point, because I once heard a certain captain severely "told off" at manoeuvres by a very senior officer for having his trenches "out of dressing." No one could tell whether some "brass hat" might not come round and inspect us next day, so it was as well to be prepared for anything.

At dusk the guard on Waschout Hill, for whom a

trench had also been dug, was relieved and increased to six men, and after teas and giving out the orders for the next day, we all "turned in" in our trenches. The tents were not pitched, as we were not going to occupy them, and it was no good merely showing up our position. A guard was mounted over our prisoners, or rather "guests," and furnished one sentry to watch over them.

Before falling asleep I ran over my seven lessons, and it seemed to me I had left nothing undone which could possibly help towards success. We were all entrenched, had a good bulletproof defence, all our rations and ammunition close at hand in the trenches, and water-bottles filled. It was with a contented feeling of having done everything right and of being quite "the little white-haired boy," that I gradually dozed off.

Next morning dawned brightly and uneventfully, and we had about an hour's work improving details of our trenches before breakfasts were ready. Just as breakfast was over, the sentry on Waschout Hill reported a cloud of dust away to the north, by Regret Table Mountain. This was caused by a large party of mounted men with wheeled transport of some sort. They were most probably the enemy, and seemed to be trekking in all innocence of our presence for the drift.

What a "scoop," I thought, if they come on quite unsuspecting, and cross the drift in a lump without discerning our position. I shall lie low, let the advanced party go past without a shot, and wait until the main body gets over the side within close range, and then open magazine fire into the thick of them. Yes, it will be just when they reach that broken anthill about 400 meters away that I shall give the word "Fire!"

However, it was not to be. After a short time the enemy halted, apparently for consideration. The advanced men seemed to have a consultation, and then gradually approached Incidentamba farm with much caution. Two or three women ran out and waved, whereupon these men galloped up to the farm at once. What passed, of course, we could not tell, but evidently the women gave information as to our arrival and position, because the effect was electrical. The advanced Boers split up into two main parties, one riding towards the river a long way to the east, and another going similarly to the west. One man galloped back with the information obtained to the main body, which became all bustle, and started off with their waggons behind Incidentamba, when they were lost to sight. Of course, they were all well out of range, and as we were quite ready, the only thing to do was to wait till they came out in the open within range, and then to shoot them down.

The minutes seemed to crawl—five, then ten minutes passed with no further sign of the enemy. Suddenly, "Beg pardon, sir; I think I see something on top of that kopje on the fur side yonder." One of the men drew my attention to a few specks which looked like waggons moving about on the flattish shoulder of Incidentamba. Whilst I was focusing my glasses there was a "boom" from the hill, followed by a sharp report and a puff of smoke up in the air quite close by, then the sound as of heavy rain pattering down some 200 feet in front of the trench, each drop raising its own little cloud of dust. This, of course, called forth the time-honoured remarks of "What ho, she bumps!"

and "Now we shan't be long," which proved only too true. I was aghast—I had quite forgotten the possibility of guns being used against me, though, had I remembered their existence, I do not know, with my then knowledge, what difference it would have made to my defensive measures. As there was some little uneasiness among my men, I, quite cheerful in the security of our nice trench with the thick bulletproof parapet, at once shouted out, "It's all right, men; keep under cover, and they can't touch us." A moment later there was a second boom, the shell whistled over our heads, and the hillside some way behind the trench was spattered with bullets.

By this time we were crouching as close as possible to the parapet, which, though it had seemed only quite a short time before so complete, now suddenly felt most woefully inadequate, with those beastly shells dropping their bullets down from the sky. Another boom. This time the shell burst well, and the whole ground in front of the trench was covered with bullets, one man being hit. At this moment rifle fire began on Waschout Will, but no bullets came our way. Almost immediately another shot followed which showered bullets all over us; a few more men were hit, whose groans were unpleasant to listen to. Tools were seized, and men began frantically to try and dig themselves deeper into the hard earth, as our trench seemed to give no more protection from the dropping bullets than a saucer would from a storm of rain—but it was too late. We could not sink into the earth fast enough. The Boers had got the range of the trench to a nicety, and the shells burst over us now with a horrible methodic precision. Several men were hit, and there was no reason why the enemy should cease to rain shrapnel over us until we were all killed. As we were absolutely powerless to do anything, I put up the white flag. All I could do was to thank Providence that the enemy had no quick-firing field guns or, though "we had not been long," we should have been blotted out before we could have hoisted it.

As soon as the gunfire ceased, I was greatly surprised to find that no party of Boers came down from their artillery position on Incidentamba to take our surrender, but within three minutes some fifty Boers galloped up from the river-bank on the east and the west, and a few more came up from the south round Waschout Hill. The guard on Waschout Hill, which had done a certain amount of damage to the enemy, had two men wounded by rifle fire. Not a single shell had come near them, though they were close to the Kaffir huts, which were plain enough.

What an anti-climax the reality had been from the pleasurable anticipations of the early morn, when I had first sighted the Boers.

Of course, the women on the farm had betrayed us, but it was difficult to make out why the Boers had at first halted and begun to be suspicious before they had seen the women at the farm. What could they have discovered? I failed entirely to solve this mystery.

During the day's trek the following lessons slowly evolved themselves, and were stored in my mind in addition to those already learnt:

8. When collecting the friendly stranger and his sons in order to prevent their taking informa-

tion to the enemy of your existence and whereabouts, if you are wishful for a "surprise packet,"
do not forget also to gather his wife and his
daughter, his manservant and his maidservant
(who also have tongues), and his ox and his
ass (which may possibly serve the enemy). Of
course, if they are very numerous or very far
off, this is impossible; only do not then hope to
surprise the enemy.

9.  Do not forget that, if guns are going to be used
against you, a shallow trench with a low parapet
some way from it is worse than useless, even
though the parapet be bulletproof ten times
over. The trench gives the gunners an object to
lay on, and gives no protection from shrapnel.
Against well-aimed long-range artillery fire it
would be better to scatter the defenders in the
open hidden in grass and bushes, or behind
stones or anthills, than to keep them huddled in
such a trench. With your men scattered around,
you can safely let the enemy fill your trench to
the brim with shrapnel bullets.

10.  Though to stop a shrapnel bullet much less actual thickness of earth is necessary than to stop
a rifle bullet, yet this earth must be in the right
place. For protection you must be able to get
right close under the cover. As narrow a trench
as possible, with the sides and inside of the
parapet as steep as they will stand, will give you
the best chance. To hollow out the bottom of
the trench sides to give extra room will be even
better, because the open top of the trench can

be kept the less wide. The more like a mere slit the open top of the trench is, the fewer shrapnel bullets will get in.

While chewing over these lessons learnt from bitter experience, I had yet another dream.

# FOURTH DREAM

"O was some power the giftie gie us,
 To see ourselves as others see us!"

   —Burns

Again did I find myself facing the same problem, this time with ten lessons to guide me. I started off by sending our patrols as described in my last dream, but their orders were slightly different. All human beings were to be brought into our post, and any animals which could be of use to the enemy were to be shot, as we had no place for them.

For my defensive post I chose the position already described in my last dream, which seemed very suitable, for the reasons already given. We consequently dug a trench similar in plan to that already described, but, as I feared the possibility of guns being used against us, it was of a very different section. In plan it faced north generally, and was slightly broken forward to the front, each half being quite straight. In section it was about three feet six inches deep, with a parapet about twelve inches high in front of it; we made the trench as narrow as possible at the top compatible with free movement. Each man hollowed out the under part of the trench to suit himself, and made his own portion of the parapet to suit his height. The parapet was about two feet six inches thick at the top and quite steep inside, being built up of pieces of broken anthill, which were nearly as hard as stone.

**Map 5**

The patrols returned shortly with their bag of a few men, women and children. The women indulged in much useless abuse, and refused to obey orders, taking the matter less philosophically than their mankind. Here was evidently an opportunity of making use of the short training I had once had as an A.D.C. I tried it. I treated the ladies with tons of "'tact" in my suavest manner, and repeated the only Dutch words of comfort I knew "Wacht een beetje"—"Al zal rech kom"—but to no purpose.

They had not been brought up to appreciate tact; in fact, they were not taking any. I turned regretfully round to the colour-sergeant, winked solemnly and officially, and seeing an answering but respectful quiver in his left eyelid, said—

"Colour-sergeant."

"Sir?"

"Which do you think is the best way of setting alight to a farm?"

"Well, sir, some prefer the large bedstead and straw, but I think the 'armonium and a little kerosene in one corner is as neat as anything."

There was no need for more. The ladies quite understood this sort of tact; the trouble was over.

The Dutchmen and Kaffirs were at once started digging shelters for themselves and the women and children. The latter were placed together, and were put into a small ravine not far from the trench, as it was necessary to place them in a really deep trench, firstly to keep them safe, and secondly to prevent their waving or signalling to the enemy. The existence of this ravine, therefore, saved much digging, as it only required some hollowing out at the bottom and a little excavation to suit admirably.

All dug with a will, and by night the shelters for the women and children, men prisoners, and the firing trench, were nearly done. All arrangements for the guards and sentries were the same as those described in the last dream, and after seeing everything was all correct and the ladies provided with tents to crawl under (they had their own blankets), I went to sleep with a feeling of well-earned security.

At daybreak next morning, as there were no signs of

any enemy, we continued to improve our trench, alter-
ing the depth and alignment where necessary, each man
suiting the size of the trench to his own legs. In the end
the trench looked quite neat—"almost as nice as mother
makes it"—with the fresh red earth contrasting with the
yellow of the veld. As one of my reservists remarked, it
only wanted an edging of oyster shells or gingerbeer
bottles to be like his little broccoli patch at home. Upon
these important details and breakfast a good two hours
had been spent, when a force was reported to the north
in the same position as described in the previous dream.
It advanced in the same manner, except, of course, the
advanced men were met by no one at the farm. When I
saw this, I could not help patting myself on the back and
smiling at the Dutch ladies in the pit, who only scowled
at me in return, and (whisper) spat!

The advanced party of the enemy came on, scouting
carefully and stalking the farm as they came. As they
appeared quite unwarned, I was wondering if I should
be able to surprise them, all innocent of our presence,
with a close-range volley, and then magazine fire into
their midst, when suddenly one man stopped and the
others gathered round him. This was when they were
some 1800 meters away, about on a level with the end
of Incidentamba. They had evidently seen something
and sniffed danger, for there was a short palaver and
much pointing. A messenger then galloped back to the
main body, which turned off behind Incidentamba with
its waggons, etc. A small number, including a man on
a white horse, rode off in a vague way to the west. The
object of this move I could not quite see. They appeared
to have a vehicle with them of some sort. The advanced

party split up as already described. As all were still at long range, we could only wait.

Very shortly "boom" went a gun from the top of Incidentamba, and a shrapnel shell burst not far from us. A second and third followed, after which they soon picked up our range exactly, and the shells began to burst all about us; however, we were quite snug and happy in our nice deep trench, where we contentedly crouched. The waste of good and valuable shrapnel shell by the enemy was the cause of much amusement to the men, who were in great spirits, and, as one of them remarked, were "as cosy as cockroaches in a crack." At the expenditure of many shells only two men were hit—in the legs.

After a time the guns ceased fire, and we at once manned the parapet and stood up to repel an attack, but we could see no Boers though the air began at once to whistle and hum with bullets. Nearly all these seemed to come from the river-bank in front, to the north and northeast, and kept the parapet one continual spurt of dust as they smacked into it. All we could do was to fire by sound at various likely bushes on the river-bank, and this we did with the greatest possible diligence, but no visible results.

In about a quarter of an hour, we had had five men shot through the head, the most exposed part. The mere raising of a head to fire seemed to be absolutely fatal, as it had on a former occasion when we were attempting to fire at close range over a parapet against the enemy concealed. I saw two poor fellows trying to build up a pitiful little kind of house of cards with stones and pieces of anthill through which to fire. This was as conspicuous as a chimney-pot on top of the parapet, and was at once shot to powder before they had even used it, but not before it had suggested to me the remedy for this state of affairs. Of course, we wanted in such a case "head cover" and "loopholes." As usual, I was wise after the event, for we had no chance of making them then, even had we not been otherwise busy. Suddenly the noise of firing became much more intense, but with the smack of the bullets striking the earth all round quite close it was not easy to tell from which direction this fresh firing came. At the same time the men seemed to be dropping much oftener, and I was impressing them with the necessity of keeping up a brisker fire to the front, when I noticed a bullet hit our side of the parapet.

It then became clear, the enemy must evidently have got into the donga behind us (to which I had paid no attention, as it was to the rear), and were shooting us in the back as we stood up to our parapet.

This, I thought, must be what is called being "taken in reverse," and it was.

By the time I had gathered what was happening, about a dozen more men had been bowled over. I then ordered the whole lot to take cover in the trench, and only to pop up to take a shot to the front or rear. But no more could be done by us towards the rear than to the front. The conditions were the same—no Boers to be seen. At this moment two of the guard from Waschout Hill started to run in to our trench, and a terrific fusillade was opened on to them, the bullets kicking up the dust all round them as they ran. One poor fellow was dropped, but the other managed to reach our trench and fall into it. He too was badly hit, but just had the strength to gasp out that except himself and the man who started with him, all the guard on Waschout Hill had been killed or wounded and that the Boers were gradually working their way up to the top. This was indeed cheering.

So hot was the fire now that no one could raise his head above ground without being shot, and by crouching down altogether and not attempting to aim, but merely firing our rifles over the edge of the trench, we remained for a short time without casualties. This respite, however, was short, for the men in the right half of the trench began to drop unaccountably whilst they were sitting well under cover, and not exposing themselves at all. I gradually discovered the cause of this. Some snipers must have reached the top of Waschout Hill, and were shooting straight down our right half trench. As the bullets snicked in thicker and thicker, it was plain the number of snipers was being increased.

This, I thought, must be being "enfiladed from a flank." It was so.

Without any order, we had all instinctively vacated the right half of our trench and crowded into the left half, which by great good luck could not be enfiladed from any point on the south side of the river, nor indeed by rifle fire from anywhere, as, owing to the ground, its prolongation on the right was up above ground for some 3000 meters away on the veld on the north bank.

Though we were huddled together quite helpless like rats in a trap, still it was in a small degree comforting to think that, short of charging, the enemy could do nothing. For that we fixed bayonets and grimly waited. If they did make an assault, we had bayonets, and they had not, and we could sell our lives very dearly in a rough-and-tumble.

Alas! I was again deceived. There was to be no chance of close quarters and cold steel, for suddenly we heard, far away out on the veld to the north, a sound as of some-one beating a tin tray, and a covey of little shells whistled into the ground close by the trench; two of these burst on touching the ground. Right out of rifle-range, away on the open veld on the north, I saw a party of Boers, with a white horse and a vehicle. Then I knew. But how had they managed to hit off so well the right spot to go to enfilade our trench before they even knew where we were?

Pom-pom pom-pom-pom again, and the little steel devils ploughed their way into the middle of us in our shell-trap, mangling seven men. I at once diagnosed the position with great professional acumen; we were now enfiladed from both flanks, but the knowledge was acquired too late to help us, for—

"We lay bare as the paunch of the purser's sow,
To the hail of the Nordenfeldt."

This was the last straw; there was nothing left but surrender or entire annihilation at long range. I surrendered.

Boers, as usual, sprang up from all round. We had fought for three hours, and had 25 killed and 17 wounded. Of these, seven only had been hit by the shrapnel and rifle fire from the front. All the rest had been killed or hit from the flanks, where there should be few en-emies, or the rear, where there should be none! This fact convinced me that my preconceived notions as to the front, and its danger relative to the other points of the compass, needed considerable modification. All my cherished ideas were being ruthlessly swept away, and I was plunged into a sea of doubt, groping for something certain or fixed to lay hold of. Could Longfellow, when he wrote that immortal line, "Things are not what they seem," ever have been in my position?

The survivors were naturally a little disheartened at their total discomfiture, when all had started so well with them in their "crack." This expressed itself in different ways. As one man said to a corporal, who was plugging a hole in his ear with a bit of rag—

"Something sickening, I call it, this enfilading racket; you never know which way it will take yer. I'm fairly fed up." To which the gloomy reply, "Enfiladed? Of course we've been enfiladed. This 'ere trench should have been wiggled about a bit, and then there would not have been quite so much of it. Yes, wiggled about—that's what it should have been." To which chipped in a third, "Yes, and something to keep the blighters from shooting us in the back wouldn't 'ave done us much 'arm, anyway."

There were evidently more things in earth than I had hitherto dreamt of in my philosophy!

As we trekked away to the north under a detached guard of Boers, many little points such as the above sank into my soul, but I could not for some time solve the mystery of why we had not succeeded in surprising the enemy. There were no men, women, children, or Kaffirs who, knowing of our arrival, could have warned them. How did they spot our presence so soon, as they evidently must have done when they stopped and consulted in the morning? It was not until passing Incidentamba, as I casually happened to look round and survey the

scene of the fight from the enemy's point of view, that
I discovered the simple answer to the riddle. There on
the smooth yellow slope of the veld just south of the
drift was a brownish-red streak, as conspicuous as the
Long Man of Wilmington on the dear old Sussex downs,
which positively shrieked aloud, "Hi! Hi! Hi!—this way
for the British defence." I then grimly smiled to think
of myself sitting like a "slick Alick" in that poster of a
trench and expecting to surprise anybody!

Besides having been enfiladed and also taken in reverse, we had again found ourselves at a disadvantage as
compared with the concealed enemy shooting at close
range, from having to show up at a fixed place in order
to fire.

Eventually I collected the following lessons—

11. For a small isolated post and an active enemy,
    there are no flanks, no rear, or, to put it other-
    wise, it is front all round.

12. Beware of being taken in reverse; take care,
    when placing and making your defences, that
    when you are engaged in shooting the enemy to
    the front of your trench, his pal cannot sneak up
    and shoot you in the back.

13. Beware of being enfiladed. It is nasty from one
    flank—far worse from both flanks.

    Remember, also, that though you may ar-
    range matters so that you cannot be enfiladed
    by rifle fire, yet you may be open to it from long
    range, by means of gun or pompom fire. There
    are few straight trenches that cannot be enfi-
    laded from somewhere, if the enemy can only

get there. You can sometimes avoid being enfiladed by so placing your trench that no one can
get into prolongation of it to fire down it, or you
can "wiggle" it about in many ways, so that it is
not straight, or make "traverses" across it, or dig
separate trenches for every two or three men.

14. Do not have your trench near rising ground
over which you cannot see, and which you cannot hold.

15. Do not huddle all your men together in a small
trench like sheep in a pen. Give them air.

16. As once before—cover from sight is often worth
more than cover from bullets.

    For close shooting from a non-concealed
trench, head cover with loopholes is an advantage. This should be bulletproof and not be
conspicuously on the top of the parapet, so as
to draw fire, or it will be far more dangerous
than having none.

17. To surprise the enemy is a great advantage.

18. If you wish to obtain this advantage, conceal
your position. Though for promotion it may be
sound to advertise your position, for defence it
is not.

19. To test the concealment or otherwise of your
position, look at it from the enemy's point of
view.

# FIFTH DREAM

"A trifling sum of misery
New added to the foot of thy account."

   —Dryden

"Jack Frost looked forth one still clear night,
And he said, 'Now I shall be out of sight,
So over the valley and over the height
In silence I'll take my way.'"

   —Gould

Again I faced the same task with a fresh mind and fresh hopes, all that remained with me of my former attempts being 19 lessons.

Having detailed the two patrols and the guard on Waschout Hill as already described, I spent some 20 minutes—whilst the stores, etc., were being arranged—in walking about to choose a position to hold in the light of my 19 lessons.

I came to the conclusion that it was not any good being near the top of a hill and yet not at the top. I would make my post on the top of Waschout Hill, where I could not be overlooked from any place within rifle range, and where I should, I believed, have "command." I was not quite certain what "command" meant, but I knew it was important—it says so in the book, besides, in all the manoeuvres I had attended and tactical schemes I had seen, the "defence" always held a position on top of a hill or ridge. My duty was plain: Waschout Hill seemed the only place which did not contravene any of the 19 lessons I had learnt, and up it I walked. As I stood near one of the huts, I got an excellent view of the drift and its southern approach just over the bulge of the hill, and a clear view of the river further east and west. I thought at first I would demolish the few grass and matting huts which, with some empty kerosene tins and heaps of bones and debris, formed the Kaffir kraal; but on consideration I decided to play cunning, and that this same innocent-looking Kaffir kraal would materially assist me to hide my defences. I made out my plan of operations in detail, and we had soon conveyed all our stores up to the top of the hill, and started work.

Upon the return of the patrols with their prisoners, the Dutchmen and "boys" were told off to dig for them-selves and their females. The Kaffirs of the kraal we had impressed to assist at once.

My arrangements were as follows: All round the huts on the hilltop and close to them, we dug some ten short lengths of deep-firing trenches, curved in plan, and each long enough to hold five men. These trenches had extremely low parapets, really only serving as rifle rests, some of the excavated earth being heaped up behind the trenches to the height of a foot or so, the remainder being dealt with as described later. In most cases the parapets were provided with grooves to fire through at ground-level, the parapet on each side be-ing high enough to just protect the head. As with the background the men's heads were not really visible, it was unnecessary to provide proper loopholes, which would have necessitated also the use of new sandbags,

**Map 6**

which would be rather conspicuous and troublesome
to conceal. When the men using these trenches were
firing, their heads would be just above the level of the
ground. Once these firing trenches were well under way,
the communication trenches were started. These were
to be narrow and deep, leading from one trench to the
next, and also leading from each trench back to four of
the huts, which were to be arranged as follows, to allow

men to fire standing up without being seen. Round the inside of the walls of these huts part of the excavated earth, of which there was ample, would be built up with sandbags, pieces of anthill, stones, etc., to a height that a man can fire over, about four and a half feet, and to a thickness of some two and a half feet at the top, and loopholes, which would be quite invisible, cut through the hut sides above this parapet. There was room in each hut for three men to fire. In three of them I meant to place my best shots, to act as snipers, as they would have a more favourable position than the men in the trenches below, and the fourth was a conning-tower for myself. All the tents and stores were stacked inside one of the huts out of sight.

That evening, in spite of the hardness of the work, which caused much grousing among my men, we had got the firing trenches complete, but the others were not finished—they were only half the necessary depth. The earth walls inside the huts were also not quite completed. The Kaffirs and Dutch had deep pits, as before, in three of the huts. Ammunition and rations were distributed round the trenches the last thing before we turned in. I also had all water-bottles and every vessel that would hold water, such as empty tins, Kaffir gourds, and cooking-pots, filled and distributed in case of a long and protracted fight. Having issued orders as to the necessity for the greatest secrecy in not giving away our position should Boers turn up early next morning, I went to sleep with confidence. We had, anyhow, a very good position, and though our communications were not perfect quite, these we could soon improve if we had any time to ourselves the next morning.

Next morning broke; no enemy in sight. This was excellent, and before daylight we were hard at it, finishing the work still undone. By this time the men had fully entered into the spirit of the thing, and were quite keen on surprising Brother Boer if possible. While the digging was proceeding, the "dixies" were being boiled for the breakfasts inside four grass screens, some of which we found lying about, so as to show nothing but some very natural smoke above the kraal. I picked out one or two of my smartest NCOs, and instructed them to walk down the hill in different directions to the river-bank and try if they could see the heads of the men in the firing trenches against the sky. If so, the heaps of earth, tins, bones, grass, screens, etc., should be rearranged so as to give a background to every man's head.

To review the place generally, I and my orderly walked off some half-mile to the north of the river. As we were going some distance, we doffed our helmets and wrapped ourselves in two beautiful orange and magenta striped blankets, borrowed from our Kaffir lady guests, in case any stray Boer should be lurking around, as he might be interested to see two "khakis" wandering about on the veld. It was awkward trying to walk with our rifles hidden under our blankets, and, moreover, every two minutes we had to look round to see if the sentry at the camp had signalled any enemy in sight. This was to be done by raising a pole on the highest hut. The result of our work was splendid. We saw a Kaffir kraal on a hill, and to us "it was nothing more." There were the heaps of debris usually round a kraal, looking most natural, but no heads were visible, and no trenches. There was only one fault, and that was that a few thoughtless men began, as we looked, to spread their brown army blankets out in the sun on top of the huts and on the veld. To the veriest new chum these square blots, like squares of brown sticking-plaster all around the kraal, would have betokened something unusual. To remedy this before it was too late I hastened back.

After we had done our breakfasts, and some three hours after dawn, the sentry in one of the huts reported a force to the north. We could do nothing but wait and hope; everything was ready, and every man knew what to do. No head was to be raised nor a rifle fired until I whistled from conning-tower; then every man would pop up and empty his magazine into any of the enemy in range. If we were shelled, the men in the huts could at once drop into the deep trenches and be safe. Standing in my conning-tower, from the loopholes of which I could see the drift, I thought over the possibilities before us. With great luck perhaps the Boer scouts would pass us on either side, and so allow us to lie low for the main body. With a view to seeing exactly how far I would let the latter come before opening fire, and to marking the exact spot when it would be best to give the word, I got down into the firing trenches facing the drift and the road south to see how matters appeared from the level of the rifles. To my intense horror, I found that from these trenches neither the drift nor the road on the near bank of the river, until it got a long way south of Waschout Hill, could be seen! The bulging convexity of the hill hid all this; it must be dead ground! It was. The very spot where I could best catch the enemy, where they must pass, was not under my fire! At most, the northern loopholes of the conning-tower and one other hut alone could give fire on the drift. How I cursed my stupidity! However, it was no-good. I could not now start digging fresh trenches further down the hill; it would betray our whole position at once. I determined to make the best of it and, if we were not discovered by the scouts, to open fire on the main body when they were just on the other side of the river bunched up on the bank, waiting for those in front. Here we could fire on them; but it would be at a much longer range than I had intended. It was really a stroke of luck that I had discovered this serious fault, for otherwise we might have let the bulk of the enemy cross the drift without discovering the little fact of the dead ground till too late. I reflected, also (though it was not much consolation), that I had erred in good company, for how often had I not seen a "brass-hat" ride along on horseback, and from that height, fix the exact position for trenches in which the rifles would be little above the ground. These trenches, however, had not been put to the test of actual use. My error was not going to escape the same way.

Meanwhile the enemy's scouts had advanced in much the same way as detailed before, except that after coming past Incidentamba Farm, they had not halted suspiciously, but came on in small groups or clumps. They crossed the river in several places and examined the bushy banks most carefully, but finding no "khakis" there, they evidently expected none on the open veld beyond them, for they advanced "anyway" without care. Several of the clumps joined together, and came on chatting in one body of some 30 men. Would they examine the kraal, or would they pass on? My heart pounded. The little hill we were on would, unluckily, be certain to prove an attraction for them, because it was an excellent vantage ground whence to scan the horizon to the south, and to signal back to the main body to the north. The kraal was also a suitable place to off-saddle for a few minutes while the main body came up to the drift, and it meant possibly a fire, and therefore a cup of coffee. They rode up towards it laughing, chatting, and smoking quite unsuspectingly. We uttered no sound. Our Dutch and Kaffir guests uttered no sound either, for in their pits was a man with a rifle alongside them. At last they halted a moment some 250 meters away on the northeast, where the slope of the hill was more gradual and showed them all up. A few dismounted, the rest started again straight towards us. It was not magnificent, but it was war. I whistled.

About ten of them succeeded in galloping off, also some loose horses; five or six of them on the ground threw up their hands and came into the post. On the ground there remained a mass of kicking horses and dead or groaning men. The other parties of scouts to east and west had at once galloped back to the river where they dismounted under cover and began to pepper us. Anyway, we had done something.

As soon as our immediate enemy were disposed of, we opened fire on the main body some 1500 meters away, who had at once halted and opened out. To these we did a good deal of damage, causing great confusion, which was comforting to watch. The Boer in command of the main body must have gathered that the river-bed was clear, for he made a very bold move; he drove the whole of the waggons, etc., straight on as fast as possible over the odd 400 meters to the river and down the drift into the river-bed, where they were safe from our fire. Their losses must have been heavy over this short distance, for they had to abandon two of their waggons on the way to the river. This was done under cover of the fire from a large number of riflemen, who had at once galloped up to the river-bank, dismounted, and opened fire at us, and from two guns and a pompom, which had immediately been driven a short distance back and then outwards to the east and west. It was really the best thing he could have done, and if he had only known that we could not fire on the ground to the south of the drift, he might have come straight on with a rush.

We had so far scored; but now ensued a period of stalemate. We were being fired at from the river-bank on the north, and from anthills, etc., pretty well all round, and were also under the intermittent shell fire from the two guns. They made most excellent practice at the huts, which were soon knocked to bits, but not till they had well served their turn. Some of the new white sandbags from inside the huts were scattered out in full view of the enemy, and it was instructive to see what a splendid target they made, and how often they were hit. They must have drawn a lot of fire away from the actual trenches. Until the Boers discovered that they could advance south from the drift without being under rifle fire from our position, they were held up.

Would they discover it? As they had ridden all round us, by now, well out of range, they must know all about us and our isolation.

After dark, by which time we had one man killed and two wounded, the firing died away into a continuous but desultory rifle fire, with an occasional drop-

ping shell from the guns. Under cover of dark, I tried
to guard the drift and dead ground to the south of it,
by making men stand up and fire at that level; but towards midnight I was forced to withdraw them into the
trenches, after several casualties, as the enemy then apparently woke up and kept up a furious rifle fire upon
us for over an hour. During this time the guns went
through some mysterious evolutions. At first we got it
very hot from the north, where the guns had been all
along. Then suddenly a gun was opened on us away
from the southwest, and we were shelled for a short
time from both sides. After a little while the shelling on
the north ceased, and continued from the southwest
only for 20 minutes. After this the guns ceased, and
the rifle fire also gradually died away.

When day dawned not a living soul was to be seen;
there were the dead men, horses, and the deserted waggons. I feared a trap, but gradually came to the conclusion the Boers had retired. After a little we discovered
the river-bed was deserted as well, but the Boers had
not retired. They had discovered the dead ground, and
under the mutually supporting fire of their guns, which
had kept us to our trenches, had all crossed the drift and
trekked south!

True, we were not captured, and had very few losses,
and had severely mauled the enemy, but they had crossed
the drift. It must have evidently been of great importance
to them to go on, or they would have attempted to capture us, as they were about 500 to our 50.

I had failed in my duty.

During the next few hours we buried the dead, tended
the wounded, and took some well-earned rest, and I had

ample leisure to consider my failure and the causes. The lessons I derived from the fight were:

20. Beware of convex hills and dead ground. Especially take care to have some place where the enemy must come under your fire. Choose the exact position of your firing trenches, with your eye at the level of the men who will eventually use them.
21. A hill may not, after all, though it has "command," necessarily be the best place to hold.
22. A conspicuous "bluff" trench may cause the enemy to waste much ammunition, and draw fire away from the actual defences.

In addition to these lessons, another little matter on my mind was what my colonel would say at my failure.

Lying on my back, looking up at the sky, I was trying to get a few winks of sleep myself before we started to improve our defences against a possible further attack, but it was no use, sleep evaded me.

The clear blue vault of heaven was suddenly overcast by clouds which gradually assumed the frowning face of my colonel. "What? You mean to say, Mr. Forethought, the Boers have crossed?" But, luckily for me, before more could be said, the face began slowly to fade away like that of the Cheshire puss in *Alice in Wonderland*, leaving nothing but the awful frown across the sky. This too finally dissolved, and the whole scene changed. I had another dream.

# SIXTH DREAM

"Sweet are the uses of adversity."

Once more was I fated to essay the task of defending Duffer's Drift. This time I had 22 lessons under my belt to help me out, and in the oblivion of my dream I was spared that sense of monotony which by now may have possibly have overtaken you, "gentle reader."

After sending out the patrols, and placing a guard on Waschout Hill, as already described, and whilst the stores were being collected, I considered deeply what position I should take up, and walked up to the top of Waschout Hill to spy out the land. On the top I found a Kaffir kraal, which I saw would assist me much as concealment should I decide to hold this hill. This I was much inclined to do, but after a few minutes' trial of the shape of the ground, with the help of some men walking about down below, and my eyes a little above ground level, I found that its convexity was such that, to see and fire on the drift and approach on the south side, I should have to abandon the top of the hill, and so the friendly concealment of the Kaffir huts, and take up a position on the open hillside some way down. This was, of course, quite feasible, especially if I held a position at the top of the hill as well, near the huts on the east and southeast sides; but, as it would be impossible to really conceal ourselves on the bare hillside, it meant giving up all idea of surprising the enemy, which I wished to do. I must, therefore, find some other place which would lend itself to easy and good concealment, and also have the drift or its approaches under close rifle fire. But where to find such a place?

As I stood deep in thought, considering this knotty problem, an idea gently wormed itself into my mind which I at once threw out again as being absurd and out of the question. This idea was to hold the river-bed and banks on each side of the drift! To give up all idea of command, and, instead of seeking the nearest high ground, which comes as natural to the student of tactics as rushing for a tree does to a squirrel, to take the lowest ground, even though it should be all among thick cover, instead of being nicely in the open.

No, it was absolutely revolutionary, and against every canon I had ever read or heard of; it was evidently the freak of a sorely tried and worried brain. I would have none of it, and I put it firmly from me. But the more I argued to myself the absurdity of it, the more this idea obtained possession of me. The more I said it was impossible, the more allurements were spread before me in its favour, until each of my conscientious objections was enmeshed and smothered in a network of specious reasons as to the advantages of the proposal.

I resisted, I struggled, but finally fell to temptation, dressed up in the plausible guise of reason. I would hold the river-bed. The advantages I thus hoped to obtain were:

1. Perfect concealment and cover from sight.
2. Trenches and protection against both rifle and gunfire practically ready made.
3. Communications under good cover.

4. The enemy would be out in the open veld
   except along the river-bank, where we,
   being in position first, would still have the
   advantage.
5. Plentiful water supply at hand.

True, there were a few dead animals near the drift, and
the tainted air seemed to hang heavy over the river-bed,
but the carcasses could be quickly buried under the steep
banks, and, after all, one could not expect every luxury.

As our clear field of fire, which in the north was only
bounded by the range of our rifles, was on the south
limited by Waschout Hill, a suitable position for the
enemy to occupy, I decided to hold the top of it as well
as the river-bed. All I could spare for this would be two
NCOs and eight men, who would be able to defend
the south side of the hill, the north being under our fire
from the river-bank.

Having detailed this party, I gave my instructions for
the work, which was soon started. In about a couple of
hours the patrols returned with their prisoners, which
were dealt with as before. For the post on Waschout Hill,
the scheme was that the trenches should be concealed
much in the same way as described in the last dream,
but great care should be taken that no one in the post
should be exposed to rifle fire from our main position
in the river. I did not wish the fire of the main body
to be in any degree hampered by a fear of hitting the
men on Waschout Hill, especially at night. If we knew
it was not possible to hit them, we could shoot freely
all over the hill. This detachment was to have a double
lot of water-bottles, besides every available receptacle

**Map 7**

collected in the kraal, filled with water, in anticipation of a prolonged struggle.

The general idea for the main defensive position was to hold both sides of the river, improving the existing steep banks and ravines into rifle-pits to contain from one to four men. These could, with very little work, be made to give cover from all sides. As such a large amount of the work was already done for us, we were enabled to dig many more of these pits than the exact number required for our party. Pathways leading between these were to be cut into the bank, so that we should be able to shift about from one position to another. Besides the advantage this would give us in the way of moving about, according as we wished to fire, it also meant that we should probably be able to mislead the enemy as to our numbers—which, by such shifting tactics might, for a time at least, be much exaggerated. The pits for fire to the north and south were nearly all so placed as to allow the occupants to fire at ground level over the veld. They were placed well among the bushes, only just sufficient scrub being cut away to allow a man to see all round, without exposing the position of his trench. On each side of the river, just by the drift, were some "spoil" heaps of earth, excavated from the road ramp. These stood some five or six feet above the general level, and were as rough as the banks in outline. These heaps were large enough to allow a few pits being made on them, which had the extra advantage of height. In some of the pits, to give head-cover, loopholes of sandbags were made, though in most cases this was not needed, owing to the concealment of the bushes. I found it was necessary to examine personally every loophole, and correct the numerous mistakes made in their construction. Some had the new clean sandbags exposed to full view, thus serving as mere whited sepulchres to their occupants, others were equally conspicuous from their absurd cock-shy appearance, others were not bullet-proof, whilst others again would only allow of shooting in one direction, or into the ground at a few meters range, or up into the blue sky. As I corrected all these faults

I thought that loopholes not made under supervision might prove rather a snare.

The result was, in the way of concealment, splendid. From these pits with our heads at ground level we could see quite clearly out on to the veld beyond, either from under the thicker part of the bushes or even through those which were close to our eyes. From the open, on the other hand, we were quite invisible, even from 300 meters distance, and would have been more so had we had the whiskers of the "brethren." It was quite evident to me that these same whiskers were a wise precaution of nature for this very purpose, and part of her universal scheme of protective mimicry.

The numerous small dongas and rifts lent themselves readily to flanking fire, and in many places the vertical banks required no cutting in order to give ideal protection against even artillery. In others, the sides of the crooked waterways had to be merely scooped out a little, or a shelf cut to stand upon.

In one of these deeper ravines two tents, which, being below ground level, were quite invisible, were pitched for the women and children, and small caves cut for them in case of a bombardment. The position extended for a length of some 150 meters on each side of the drift along both banks of the river, and at its extremities, where an attack was most to be feared, pits were dug down the river-banks and across the dry river-bed. These also were concealed as well as possible. The flanks or ends were, of course, our greatest danger, for it was from here we might expect to be rushed, and not from the open veld. I was undecided for some time as to whether to clear a "field of fire" along the river-banks or not, as I had no wish to give away our presence by any suspicious nudity of the banks at each end of our position. I finally decided, in order to prevent this, to clear the scrub for as great a range as possible from the ends of the position, everywhere below the ground level, and also on the level ground, except for a good fringe just on the edges of the banks. This fringe I thought would be sufficient to hide the clearance to any one not very close. I now blessed the man who had left us some cutting tools. Whilst all this was being carried out, I paced out some ranges to the north and south, and these we marked by a few empty tins placed on ant-heaps, etc.

At dusk, when we had nearly all the pits finished and some of the clearance done, tents and gear were hidden, ammunition and rations distributed to all, and orders in case of an attack given out. As I could not be everywhere, I had to rely on the outlying groups of men fully under-standing my aims beforehand, and acting on their "own." To prevent our chance of a close-range volley into the enemy being spoilt by some over-zealous or jumpy man opening fire at long range, I gave orders that fire was to be held as long as possible, and that no man was to fire a shot until firing had already commenced elsewhere (which sounded rather Irish), or my whistle sounded. This was unless the enemy were so close to him that further silence was useless. Firing having once started, every man was to blaze away at any enemy within range as judged by our range marks. Finally we turned in to our pit for the night with some complacency, each eight men furnishing their own sentry.

We had about three hours next morning before any enemy were reported from Waschout Hill (the pre-

arranged signal for this was the raising of a pole from
one of the huts). This time was employed in perfecting
our defences in various ways. We managed to clear away
the scrub in the dry river-bed and banks for some 200
meters beyond our line of pits on each side, and actually
attained to the refinement of an "obstacle"; for at the
extremity of this clearance a sort of abatis entanglement
was made with the wire from an adjacent fence which
the men had discovered. During the morning I visited
the post on Waschout Hill, found everything all correct,
and took the opportunity of showing the detachment
the exact limits of our position in the river-bed, and
explained what we were going to do. After about three
hours work, "Somebody in sight" was signalled, and we
soon after saw from our position a cloud of dust away to
the north. This force, which proved to be a commando,
approached as already described in the last dream; all
we could do meanwhile was to sit tight in concealment.
Their scouts came in clumps of twos and threes which
extended over some mile of front, the centre of the line
heading for the drift. As the scouts got closer, the natural impulse to make for the easiest crossing place was
obeyed by two or three of the parties on each side of the
one approaching the drift, and they inclined inwards and
joined forces with it. This was evidently the largest party
we could hope to surprise, and we accordingly lay for it.
When about 300 meters away, the "brethren" stopped
rather suspiciously. This was too much for some man
on the east side, who let fly, and the air was rent by the
rattle as we emptied our magazines, killing five of this
special scouting party and two from other groups further
out on either side. We continued to fire at the scouts as

they galloped back, dropping two more, and also at the column which was about a mile away, but afforded a splendid target till it opened out.

In a very few moments our position was being shelled by three guns, but with the only result, as far we were concerned of having one man wounded by shell fire, though the firing went on slowly till dark. To be accurate, I should say the river was being shelled, our position incidentally, for shells were bursting along the river for some half-mile. The Boers were evidently quite at sea as regards to the extent of our position and strength, and wasted many shells. We noticed much galloping of men away to the east and west, out of range, and guessed that these were parties who intended to strike the river at some distance away, and gradually work along the bed, in order probably to get into close range during the night.

We exchanged a few shots during the night along the river-bed, and not much was done on either side, though of course we were on the *qui vive* all the time; but it was not till near one in the morning that Waschout Hill had an inning.

As I had hoped, the fact that we held the kraal had not been spotted by the enemy, and a large body of them, crawling up the south side of the hill in order to get a good fire on to us in the river, struck a snag in the shape of a close-range volley from our detachment. As the night was not very dark, in the panic following the first volley our men were able (as I learnt afterwards) to stand right up and shoot at the surprised burghers bolting down the hill. However, their panic did not last long, to judge by the sound, for after the first volley from our Lee-Metfords and the subsequent minutes of independent firing, the reports of our rifles were soon mingled with the softer reports of the Mausers, and we shortly observed flashes on our side of Waschout Hill. As these could not be our men, we knew the enemy was endeavouring to surround the detachment. We knew the ranges fairly well, and though, as we could not see our sights, the shooting was rather guesswork, we soon put a stop to this manoeuvre by firing a small volley from three or four rifles at each flash on the hillside. So the night passed without much incident.

During the dark we had taken the opportunity to cunningly place some new white sandbags (which I had found among the stores) in full view at some little distance from our actual trenches and pits. Some men had even gone further, and added a helmet here and a coat there peeping over the top. This ruse had been postponed until our position was discovered, so as not to betray our presence, but after the fighting had begun no harm was done by it. Next morning it was quite a pleasure to see the very accurate shooting made by "Brother" at these sandbags, as betokened by the little spurts of dust.

During this day the veld to the north and south was deserted by the enemy except at out-of-range distance, but a continuous sniping fire was kept up along the river-banks on each side. The Boer guns were shifted—one to the top of Incidentamba and one to the east and west in order to enfilade the river-bank—but, owing to our good cover, we escaped with two killed and three wounded. The enemy did not shell quite such a length of river this time. I confidently expected an attack along the river-bank that night, and slightly strengthened my flanks,

even at the risk of dangerously denuding the north bank.
I was not disappointed.

Under cover of the dark, the enemy came up to within,
perhaps, 600 meters of the open veld on the north and
round the edges of Waschout Hill on the south, and
kept up a furious fire, probably to distract our attention, whilst the guns shelled us for about an hour. As
soon as the gunfire ceased they tried to rush us along
the river-bed east and west, but, owing to the abatis and
the holes in the ground, and the fact that it was not a
very dark night, they were unsuccessful. However, it was
touch-and-go, and a few of the Boers did succeed in
getting into our position, only to be bayoneted. Luckily the enemy did not know our strength, or rather our
weakness, or they would have persisted in their attempt
and succeeded; as it was, they must have lost 20 or 30
men killed and wounded.

Next morning, with so many men out of my original
40 out of action (not to include Waschout Hill, whose
losses I did not know) matters seemed to be serious,
and I was greatly afraid that another night would be the
end of us. I was pleased to see that the detachment on
Waschout Hill had still got its sail well up, for they had
hoisted a red rag at the masthead. True, this was not
the national flag, probably only a mere handkerchief,
but it was not white. The day wore on with intermittent
shelling and sniping, and we all felt that the enemy must
have by now guessed our weakness, and were saving
themselves for another night attack, relying upon our
being tired out. We did our best to snatch a little sleep
by turns during the day, and I did all I could to keep the
spirits of the little force up by saying that relief could

not be very far off. But it was with a gloomy desperation at best that we saw the day wear on and morning turn into afternoon.

The Boer guns had not been firing for some two hours, and the silence was just beginning to get irritating and mysterious, when the booming of guns in the distance aroused us to the highest pitch of excitement. We were saved! We could not say what guns these were—they might be British or Boer—but, anyway, it proved the neighbourhood of another force. All faces lighted up, for somehow the welcome sound at once drew the tired feeling out of us.

In order to prevent any chance of the fresh force missing our whereabouts, I collected a few men and at once started to fire some good old British volleys into the scrub, "Ready—present—fire!!!" which were not to be mistaken. Shortly afterwards we heard musketry in the distance, and saw a cloud of dust to the northeast. We were relieved!

Our total losses were 11 killed and 15 wounded; but we had held the drift, and so enabled a victory to be won. I need not here touch upon the well-known and far-reaching results of the holding of Duffer's Drift, of the prevention thereby of Boer guns, ammunition, and reinforcements reaching one of their sorely pressed forces at a critical moment, and the ensuing victory gained by our side. It is now, of course, public knowledge that this was the turning point in the war, though we, the humble instruments, did not know what vital results hung upon our action.

That evening the relieving force halted at the drift, and, after burying the dead, we spent some time examining the lairs of the Boer snipers, the men collecting bits of shell and cartridge cases as mementoes—only to be thrown away at once. We found some 25 dead and partly buried Boers, to whom we gave burial.

That night I did not trek, but lay down (in my own breeches and spotted waistcoat). As the smoke from the "prime segar," presented to me by the Colonel, was eddying in spirals over my head, these gradually changed into clouds of rosy glory, and I heard brass bands in the distance playing a familiar air: "See the Conquering Hero comes," it sounded like.

I felt a rap on my shoulder, and heard a gentle voice say, "Arise, Sir Backsight Forethought"; but in a trice my dream of bliss was shattered—the gentle voice changed into the well-known croak of my servant. "Time to pack your kit on the waggon, sir. Corfy's been up some time now, sir."

I was still in stinking old Dreamdorp.

# APPENDIX

*Web Site Information*

Readers can explore aspects of 2LT Connors's mission and counterinsurgency in more depth by visiting http://www.defenseofJAD.com. This Web site contains excellent resources for both students and instructors of counterinsurgency, including

- color illustrations and graphics
- Leader Professional Development exercises based on the book
- links to counterinsurgency Web sites
- discussion boards
- author interviews

# BIBLIOGRAPHY

*Battaglia di Algeri, La.* Directed by Gillo Pontecorvo. Italy: Casbah Film, 1966.

Galula, David. *Counterinsurgency Warfare Theory and Practice.* Westport, CT: Praeger Security International, 2006.

Guevara, Ernesto. *Guerrilla Warfare.* New York: Ocean Press, 2006.

Kennedy, John. "Remarks to the Graduating Class of the United States Military Academy." West Point, NY: 1962. Accessed at http://www.jfklibrary.org/Historical+Resources/Archives/Reference+Desk/Speeches.

Kilcullen, David. "Twenty Eight Articles: Fundamentals of Company-Level Counterinsurgency." *Military Review* 86, no. 3 (May–June 2006): 103–6.

Lawrence, T. E. *Seven Pillars of Wisdom: A Triumph.* New York: Anchor Books, 1991.

———. "Twenty Seven Articles." *Arab Bulletin*, 20 August 1917.

Mao Tse-tung. *On Guerrilla Warfare.* Champaign: University of Illinois Press, 2000.

Marcus Aurelius. *The Meditations of Marcus Aurelius.* Boston: Shambhala Publications, 1993.

Marighella, Carlos. *Minimanual of the Urban Guerrilla.* Boulder, CO: Paladin Press, 1985.

Nagl, John. *Learning to Eat Soup with a Knife: Counterinsurgency Lessons from Malaya and Vietnam.* Chicago: University of Chicago Press, 2005.

———. *National Training Center Observer Controller Handbook.* Fort Irwin, CA: National Training Center, 2007.

Petraeus, David. "Learning Counterinsurgency: Observations from Soldiering in Iraq." *Military Review* 86, no. 1 (January–February 2006): 2–12.

Sun-tzu. *The Art of War.* Boulder, CO: Westview Press, 1994.

Swinton, E. D. *The Defence of Duffer's Drift.* Wayne, NJ: Avery Publishing Group, 1986.

United States Army. Field Manual 90-8, *Counterguerrilla Operations.* Washington, DC: U.S. Government Printing Office, August 1986.

———. Field Manual 3-20.98, *Reconnaissance Platoon.* Washington, DC: U.S. Government Printing Office, 2 December 2002.

United States Army and United States Marine Corps. Field Manual 3-24, *Counterinsurgency.* Washington, DC: U.S. Government Printing Office, 15 December 2006. Published under the title *The U.S. Army/Marine Corps Counterinsurgency Field Manual*, with a foreword by John A. Nagl, James F. Amos, and David H. Petraeus, and an introduction by Sarah Sewall. Chicago: University of Chicago Press, 2007.